TWO ISLANDS AND A TORTOISE

Simple History I Showed My Family About Prosperity And The Proper Role Of Government

ARI JANMOHAMED

TABLE OF CONTENTS

INTRODUCTION

● ● ● ● ● ● ● ● ● ● ●

I'm very concerned about the extreme political climate my family is living in. This book aims to provide a reasonable perspective. Before today's legislative proposals are considered, my hope is that the experience of millions who have already lived under such policies or their derivatives will be regarded above personal ideals and inherited biases. Every generation mistakenly believes their situation is the exception to the rule; that the sacrosanct lessons of success don't apply because "it's different this time," but history repeats itself.

What if we could somehow take advice from an impartial third party, a tortoise perhaps, whose extended life span affords him the credibility of first-hand accounts over a few hundred years? In reality the oldest known tortoise was said to have lived from 1750 to 2006. If such a character were inclined to share his unvarnished observations of economic progress from countries around the world with the hope of teaching those willing to heed time-tested principles, then you understand the intent of Part I of this book. Part II is a concise commentary from the same tortoise about

America's progress since its founding and the differing results he saw between government and business at the country's helm.

Ultimately, the questions we may wish this tortoise to answer would be, "How can a people best pursue prosperity, and what role does government play in that pursuit?"

PART I

THE SIX RULES OF GOVERNMENT

RULE NUMBER ONE

Once there was a group of people stranded on an island. Pirates were known to sail near the island so one day everyone gathered on the beach to talk about what to do.

Near the back of the crowd, a girl named Izzy was playing by the water. There, she found a big boulder that she hadn't seen before. Thinking there might be treasure underneath, she tried to flip it over—and a head popped out.

"Hey, that tickles!"

"Whoa!" said Izzy. "Who—or what—are you?"

"Hi, there! My name is Tommy, and I'm a tortoise. Pleased to meet you!"

"Pleased to meet you too. My name is Izzy."

"Listen, Izzy, I've been on this beach all morning and I couldn't help but overhear your island is trying to decide what to do about the pirates. I've seen a lot of other islands in your situation. Do you mind if I give you some advice?"

"Sure you can, but why not just talk to the adults over there?"

"I tried that a few years ago, but adults don't believe animals can talk, so they just stared at me . . . It was very awkward! I'd like to help you avoid the mistakes other islands have made. How about you tell the people on your island everything I tell you, and in return, I'll let you ride on my shell when I go swimming. Deal?"

"Deal!"

"OK. Well, what I'm going to tell you is what I saw other islands do over a few hundred years. Tortoises can live a long time! The islands that were protected from pirates and that always seemed to have enough food to eat followed the same six rules. What the adults on your island are talking about is forming a government."

"What's that?"

"A government is a group of people that protects your island from pirate attacks and makes sure everyone on the island obeys the same laws," the tortoise explained. "Let me show you something, Izzy."

Both Tommy and Izzy turned around to face the ocean.

"Do you see those two islands in the distance?" Tommy continued. "Both islands are empty now, but a hundred years ago, a lot of people were living there. The island on the right formed a government and established laws for everybody to follow.

The island on the left did something different. They did not form a government, so each person made up their own laws. One person made a law that only he could play on the beach during the day. Another person made a law that anyone could play on the beach whenever they wanted. It was chaos! No one obeyed the same laws and everyone began to fight with each other. So here's rule number one, Izzy: government must be centralized so the rule of law can apply to everyone."

RULE #1

Government must be centralized.

RULE #1 IN HISTORY

Secure property rights, the law, public services, and the freedom to contract and exchange all rely on the state, the institution with the coercive capacity to impose order, prevent theft and fraud, and enforce contracts between private parties...Though many of these public services can be provided by markets and private citizens, the degree of coordination necessary to do so on a large scale often eludes all but a central authority.

—Acemoglu and Robinson, *Why Nations Fail*

FOLLOWING THE RULE: The Bushong
Anything You Can Do I Can Do Better

One of the many tributaries of the Congo River is the Kasai, along which reside two tribes of people that Acemoglu and Robinson write about in *Why Nations Fail*. Along the eastern bank are the Bushong. To the west are the Lele. The river is easily crossed by boat, and both tribes are quite similar in language and culture. In the 1950s, an anthropologist studied these two tribes and noted that whatever the Lele farmed or produced was used for the tribe's survival. Meanwhile, the Bushong produced a surplus in crops that were exchanged in a market. She observed, "The Lele are poor, while the Bushong are rich…Everything that the Lele have or can do, the Bushong have more and can do better."[1]

The difference in prosperity between these two tribes can be traced back to what occurred politically around the year 1620. In that time, a man called Shyaam established himself as king, with the Bushong area at the center of the kingdom. Shyaam and his successors created a legal system and a police force to administer the law. Leaders were instructed to consult with councils before making any decisions. There was even trial by jury. One could walk around the Bushong area without fear of being attacked. Agricultural technology was adopted from the Americas. Farming included multiple crops, which were rotated every few years. Older crops were replaced by higher-yielding ones. The amount of food per capita doubled, and the Bushong enjoyed up to three harvests per year.[2]

On the other hand, Shyaam did not implement his systems on the east bank of the Kasai. The Lele were spread out in villages with no central authority. Anyone collecting food in the forest was likely kidnapped. Lele men tended to marry much later in life, devoting their youth to fighting and raiding other villages. There was no incentive to adopt better hunting and farming technologies. The Lele did not use fishing nets nor did they utilize sturdier methods to build homes. At most, the Lele tribe could expect only one harvest of maize per year.[2]

Shyaam's motivations were authoritarian, living off the surplus of his people. However, a surplus of food and wealth were produced nevertheless because of the establishment of a central government, enforcement of the law, incentives to adopt new technology, and the exchange of crop surpluses in the market.

BREAKING THE RULE: Somalia

Rebel without a Cause

The people of Somalia have historically been organized into six clan families with many subgroups. Political power was widely dispersed. Every adult man could include his input on decisions regarding the clan, but no one had any real governing power. Except for the use of Sharia law as a framework, there was no written law, no police, and no legal system. The most widely accepted rule was "blood wealth" in which a clan would be paid (usually in the form of camels) if a member of their group was killed or even injured by someone in another clan. When modern transportation reached Somalia, blood wealth still applied in motorcycle accidents.[3]

When the British arrived with hopes of colonization, law and order was impossible. There was constant feuding among the clans, and no one respected the authority of the other. The most disheartening result of Somalia's de-centralized authority and constant infighting was that the country could not adopt the technological advances brought by the British Industrial Revolution. Thus, economic progress remained non-existent, and to this day, Somalia is among the poorest countries in the world.

RULE NUMBER TWO

"I think I understand," said Izzy. "But who leads the government? Can you?"

"Well, I don't think a lot of people would follow a tortoise. See how slow I move?"

"I would follow you, Tommy."

"That's nice of you to say!"

"So where do we get a leader?"

"Leaders are chosen from among the people who live on the island," Tommy explained. "The island on my right voted to decide who would be their leader."

"What does 'vote' mean?" Izzy asked.

"It means they raised their hand when the person they liked the most started to talk. The person with the most votes was the leader, but he wasn't their leader forever. Every few years the island on the right voted again to see if they wanted to keep him as their leader."

"Why would they do that?"

"They do that so the leader will always do what's best for the island, not for himself. If they think he's not doing a good job, they could vote for someone else."

Izzy nodded in understanding.

"Now look at the island to my left. One day the strongest man on the island simply chose himself as the leader, and everyone followed him because they were afraid. He was the leader his whole life, and he did not do what was best for the island because he knew the people could not replace him. He ate most of the island's food, and he did not protect the people when the pirates attacked. Here's rule number two, Izzy: to hold their leaders accountable, the people must vote on a recurring basis."

RULE #2

The people must vote on a regular basis.

RULE #2 IN HISTORY

Should things go wrong at any time, the people will set them to rights by the peaceable exercise of their elective rights.

—Thomas Jefferson, 1806

The structure of government determines the ability of citizens to control their politicians and influence how they behave. Those governments whose officials are elected remain agents of the public, for the public can vote them out of office. Thus, the incentive exists for leaders to act on behalf of the people. However, if government officials are self-appointed and are not limited to any specific term of service, their philosophy of governance tends to be self-serving. Personal agendas,

wealth, and power are pursued at the expense of the citizenry to stay in office.

FOLLOWING THE RULE: The United States of America

Are You Better off Than Before?

Jimmy Carter became president of the United
States on January 20, 1977. The country was already in
a bad state of affairs, with high inflation, high interest rates, and high unemployment. These lackluster
economic indicators coupled with other events proved
impossible for President Carter to overcome politically.
America became very pessimistic about the future. John
F. Kennedy, his brother Robert F. Kennedy, and Martin
Luther King Jr. were all assassinated. The Vietnam
War was lost, the Watergate scandal dampened political optimism, and oil prices had skyrocketed. In 1979,
President Carter gave a nationally televised address
in which he described a "crisis of confidence" among
the American people. President Carter boycotted the
Summer Olympics in Moscow because the Soviet Union
invaded Afghanistan, and his administration admitted full responsibility for the failed rescue attempt
of hostages abroad, which resulted in the deaths of
eight servicemen.

Carter's critics saw him as an inept leader who had failed to solve worsening economic problems. With President Carter's unpopularity in Congress and the widespread blame placed upon him for national crises, the American people looked to someone else. Ronald Reagan famously asked the American people, "Are you better off than you were four years ago? Is there more or less unemployment . . . than there was four years ago?"[1] Reagan won the presidential election in a landslide. He won 489 electoral votes compared to Carter's 49 and won the popular vote by more than 8 million. Reagan's victory in 1980 made Carter the first elected president to be refused a second term since 1932.

FOLLOWING THE RULE: England

Check mate

English history is full of violent clashes between the monarchy and its subjects. In 1688 King James II of England sought to expand the power of the throne, and civil war ensued. But Parliament was prepared and invited William of Orange (a sovereign prince from the Netherlands) to replace King James II. With his army, William claimed the throne of England to rule as a "constitutional monarch" with much more influence from Parliament—the legislative body of elected officials that, until this time, had little influence over the king. Within a few months of William's arrival to the British Isles, King James fled to France.

In 1689 Parliament produced the Declaration of Rights, which were read aloud to William when he was offered the crown. The Declaration of Rights made clear that the new king could not suspend or dispense with laws. Taxation could not occur without Parliament's consent, nor would succession to the throne be automatic from William's hereditary line. Authority and decision-making power had now switched from the king to England's body of elected officials. The interests of these representatives were very different than those of kings past. Members of Parliament had an incentive to enforce property rights, given their investments in trade and industry. They raised taxes to strengthen the navy, which protected overseas mercantile interests. Previously, kings would take property away and raise taxes to enrich themselves.

BREAKING THE RULE: North Korea
Table for One

North Korea's people have long suffered poverty, starvation, human rights violations, and a ten-fold economic disparity with that of South Korea.[2] Meanwhile, dictator Kim Jong-Il and his government elites enjoyed a seven-story pleasure palace equipped with a movie

theatre, a wave pool, and a karaoke machine.[3] It is estimated Kim Jong-Il had an annual liquor budget of
$800,000.

Kim Jong-Il's son, Kim Jong-un, inherited the
dictatorship and exercises even more indifference to
the people he rules. Though the average annual income
of North Koreans is only $1,800, Kim Jong-un spends
$2,145 per bottle on his favorite liquor. He owns an $8
million yacht, $8.2 million in watches, and a private jet
named Air Force Un; he maintains seventeen different
palaces. In 2010 it was rumored he gifted a Mercedes-
Benz sedan to each of his 160 political cronies, but none
to the suffering masses abused by his regime.[4]

BREAKING THE RULE: Congo

Rumble in the Jungle

Congo became independent from Belgian colonial
rule in 1960. At the time, Joseph Mobutu was secretary
of state for national defense, but after a coup in 1965,
Mobutu took control of the government as a military dictator. Throughout his reign citizens were impoverished,
but Mobutu and the elites surrounding him grew very
wealthy. He outlawed political parties and frequently
imprisoned or executed opponents. In 1967 he issued a
new constitution, which said presidential elections were
to occur every seven years. However, of the three times

Mobutu ran for office, he corruptly garnered 99 percent of the vote.

In 1971 Mobutu began to nationalize foreign-owned companies in the region. From the two thousand companies he took over, Mobutu pocketed an estimated $5 billion without channeling that wealth to his people. He bought a luxury yacht that sailed the Congo River. He imported a massive fleet of Mercedes-Benz vehicles and flew his private plane to Paris on frequent shopping trips. He also bought several mansions in Spain, Portugal, Switzerland, and Belgium. In 1974 Mobutu hosted the famous "Rumble in the Jungle" heavyweight fight between George Foreman and Muhammad Ali. Mobutu lived a comfortable life, but the nation experienced large debt, massive inflation, poverty, and human rights violations. In 1997 rebel forces expelled Mobutu and he died three months later in Morocco.

RULE NUMBER THREE

"What if I don't like the leader that the people choose?"

"One of the laws on the island to my right was that you had to respect the majority decision—that's the person who received the most votes from the island's people—even if you disagreed. Everyone was OK with that because every few years, they had a chance to vote again for someone else."

"OK, so what does a leader do once he's chosen?"

"Once a leader is chosen, he makes sure the government does what the people need. He buys ships to defend the island against pirate attacks and he hires policemen to make sure everyone on the island obeys the laws."

"Does the leader buy the ships and pay the policemen with his own money? I couldn't do that. All I have is a few coins."

"Actually, most people are like you, Izzy! Most people don't have enough money to buy ships to fight pirates. Instead, everyone just pays a few of their coins to the govern- ment. When everybody on the island helps pay a little bit, the government ends up with enough money to buy the ships and hire the policemen that the island needs. The money you pay to the government is called 'taxes.'"

"Does everybody on the island pay taxes?"

"All the people on the island to my right paid taxes. If you were poor, you paid less. If you were rich, you paid more. But everyone had to pay something. Since everyone lived on the island, it was everyone's responsibility to help pay to keep it safe."

"That makes sense," Izzy responded.

"The island to my left did something different. Only the rich people paid taxes. The government had enough money for a while, but as more people lived on the island, the rich people had to pay more of their money to afford more ships and more policemen. Eventually, the rich people got tired of paying all their money to the government. One by one, rich people moved to another island or stopped working altogether. As a result, the government ran out of money and could no longer buy ships to fight pirates so the island was attacked. Rule number three, Izzy, is that everyone must pay taxes. The poor pay less and the rich pay more, but everybody pays something."

RULE # 3

Everyone must pay taxes.

RULE #3 IN HISTORY

In every society also there must be some taxes,
because the necessity of supporting government
and defending the state always exists. To do these
on the cheapest terms is wise...Still it would be
wise to carry taxation to a certain amount, and
expend what should remain after providing for the
support of government and the national defense
in works of public utility, such as opening of roads
and navigation.

—Robert Morris, 1782

Like children, elected officials in government produce nothing. Hence, government's survival is 100 percent dependent on the taxes it extracts from others. Since
the citizenry serve as host to this parasitic politic, taxation must be restrained lest the government's feeding

of the people's financial lifeblood becomes so excessive that the life of the host itself is threatened. Taxes, therefore, must only be used to serve the people in ways which they cannot serve themselves, such as national security and public-use infrastructure. Unfortunately, politicians view taxation as a charitable sip from another's natural cash flow stream rather than a weight that actually restricts the businessman's strength to continue pulling water from the well.

FOLLOWING THE RULE: France
All for One, and One for All

For centuries France was ruled by a monarchy and was divided into three groups. Nobility was the first, church clergy was the second, and the third group was everyone else—namely merchants, businessmen, professionals, and artisans. One of the biggest differences among these groups was that nobility and clergy did not pay taxes; everyone else did. The monarchy and the clergy enjoyed a luxurious lifestyle while most others lived in poverty. Though the feudal system was in decline, many French peasants were still required to work rural lands and pay dues to the lords. King Louis XIV, in particular, wanted to change the French tax system. France often had problems financing its frequent wars and, of course, the king's own luxurious lifestyle.

The French Revolution in 1789 changed this backdrop. On August 4, 1789, a new constitution was proposed. It abolished the feudal system and serfdom. It also stated that, "taxes shall be collected from all the citizens, and from all property, in the same manner and in the same form. Plans shall be considered by which the taxes shall be paid proportionally by all."[1] This was a radical economic and political change. With the removal of their previous system, a more level playing field was established. It is because of the French Revolution and the market-friendly policies that ensued over time that France enjoyed economic growth unseen by Austria-Hungary and Russia during the same time period.

BREAKING THE RULE: Kingdom of Kongo

Oops, I Did It Again

Another African country Acemoglu and Robinson write about is Kongo. They note that during the fifteenth and sixteenth centuries, Portuguese visitors to the Kongo observed the "miserable poverty" that existed there. Kongo was governed by the king in Mbanza, but areas away from the capital were ruled by elite governors. Slave plantations were a major part of the Kongolese economy. Excessive taxes were also a major factor in supporting the elites. There was even a tax levied when the king's beret fell off his head.[2]

The slave farmers could try to be more prosperous and sell their produce in the market, but with the king exacting arbitrary taxes to take what they already had, there was no incentive to invest in more useful tools like the plow. Instead, the Kongolese people moved their villages as far away from the capital and major roads as possible to avoid slave traders and the plundering of the king's elite governors.[2]

BREAKING THE RULE: New York and Connecticut
Climate Change

In the last decade New York has lost over a million taxpayers, many of whom moved to Florida. According to New York State Republican Chairman Nick Langworthy in an interview with FOX Business, "[The governor] has blamed the weather—but really at the end of the day it's because [other states] don't have a state income tax . . . If you look at states that are taxing less, they are growing."[3] Data from the US Census Bureau showed that while Florida received more movers than any other state in 2018, New York's outflows to the Sunshine State were the highest.[4]

New York is not alone. In the last five years, Connecticut has also lost population. Overreaching taxes continue to show themselves on annual state budgets. Recently, taxes have been proposed on Netflix movies, veterinary bills, legal services, horse boarding, nonprescription drugs, and haircuts.[5] The Connecticut legislature approved an increase on capital gains tax for individuals in the top income bracket, in 2015 the state's 7.5 percent corporate tax rate effectively rose to 9 percent, and the top income tax rate has increased three times in the past ten years. As a result, residents and businesses are protesting by moving away. General Electric left for Boston in 2016, and United Technologies Corporation, Connecticut's largest employer, announced it, too, will move its headquarters to Massachusetts.[6]

Connecticut is a sad story. It was once a haven for wealthy New Yorkers because of its nonexistent income tax, top-rated schools, and good community environment. But now the state has managed to extend the effects of the 2008 recession even during a booming US economy. The federal Bureau of Economic Analysis reported that Connecticut's gross domestic product (GDP) grew only 1 percent in 2018 while the US economy grew about 3 percent.[5] Connecticut routinely ranks near the bottom in surveys of economic competitiveness, and property values have not recovered since the 2008 market crash. Since 2015 Connecticut has lost $3.9 billion in tax revenues, with Hallmark, RBS, Bristol-Myers Squibb, Boehringer Ingelheim pharmaceuticals, and Rogers Corporation having all announced job cuts or moves.[7] Perhaps this declining economic activity isn't due to heightened taxes. Maybe the weather in all surrounding states really did get measurably better ten years ago . . .

BREAKING THE RULE: Sierra Leone

Slipping Past SLPP

In 1961 Sierra Leone became independent from British rule, and governing power was handed to the Sierra Leone People's Party (SLPP). In 1967 the SLPP lost power when the people elected Siaka Stevens. Like many post-independence leaders in Africa, Stevens was more interested in keeping his political power than growing the country's economy. One of the tools he used to stay in power was a government program initially intended to help farmers.

Prices for agricultural commodities were very volatile, and the incomes of farmers were accordingly unpredictable. The British set up the Sierra Leone Produce Marketing Board in 1949, with the intention of absorbing price fluctuations so the farmers wouldn't have to. When the prices of cocoa were high, the Marketing Board would pay farmers a little less. When cocoa prices were low, farmers would get paid a little more. Over time this program served as a vehicle to tax farmers heavily as the Board paid them less and less for their produce while keeping the difference for themselves.

By the end of Stevens's rule in 1985, farmers of palm kernels, cocoa, and coffee were only getting paid 37 percent, 19 percent, and 27 percent (respectively) of the actual price of their produce. This represented an effective tax rate as high as 81 percent![8] Stevens's government kept the money to buy political support instead of using the tax revenues to improve the country's infrastructure. Roads began to crumble away, education systems disappeared, radio towers fell over due to lack of maintenance, civil servants stopped being paid, and rebels from Liberia led by Foday Sankoh started crossing the border undeterred in 1991.

It should not be surprising that Sankoh's group, who called themselves the Revolutionary United Front (RUF), invaded Sierra Leone so easily. Stevens dismantled Sierra Leone's army and protected only himself with a small band of private security personnel. In 1992 Stevens's government was overthrown by a group of only thirty soldiers[9] but the war that followed continued until 2001. The RUF who invaded Sierra Leone committed atrocious human rights violations, mass executions, and forced labor. By the end of the war, the country's roads and buildings had been completely destroyed and an estimated eighty thousand people had died.[9]

BREAKING THE RULE: Venice

The Italian Job

In the ninth century, Venice was a nation of shipping companies that serviced the trade of spices, slaves, and other manufactured goods. Venice grew very rich, and by the fourteenth century, it was bigger than Paris and three times the size of London.[10] This economic momentum spurred political reforms, including the creation of private contracts and bankruptcy laws.

However, the new success of common entrepreneurs threatened the wealth and power of the government's elite. The Great Council, made up of judges and aristocrats nominated from among the people, was the central authority in Venice. Over time, nominations to the Great Council were closed to all outsiders and reserved only for members of the elites' families. The Great Council also banned the use of private shipping contracts—the very vehicle that made Venice so rich in the first place. In 1314 the Venetian government started to nationalize the trading industry and charged individuals high taxes if they wanted to do business.[10] Trade routes were now effectively the business of nobility and no longer that of the common man.

While the population of Europe expanded at high rates from 1650 to the 1800s, that of Venice shrunk. People no longer had incentives to participate in Venice's economy. As Acemoglu and Robinson quipped, Venice today is best known for tourism and good pizza instead of the worldwide financial hub it started out to be.

RULE NUMBER FOUR

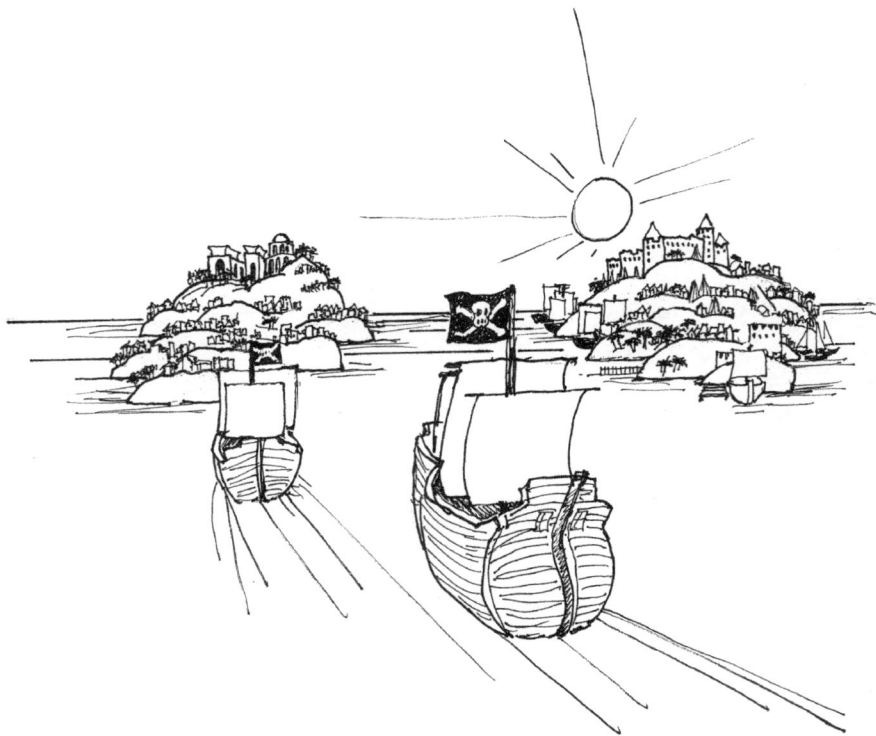

"Can the government use taxes to buy other things for me? What if I want a new surfboard or a fishing pole?"

"From all the islands I've seen, Izzy, governments will always have enough money to protect you but tend to run out of money if they try to do anything more. Remember what the island on the right did? Everyone paid taxes and the government had enough money to buy ships to fight pirates. But if the government buys other things like surfboards and fishing poles for people, too, they will run out of money."

"Can't the people just pay more taxes?"

"If the people have money to pay more taxes, they might as well keep the money to buy the things they wanted in the first place without giving it to the government, right?"

"Yeah, I guess that makes sense. OK, so what if I don't have enough money to buy what I want?"

"Well, how do your parents buy what they want?"

"With the money they earn from work, I think."

"That's right! You can buy anything you want as long as you earn the money to buy it yourself. That way the government has enough money to protect you from pirates. If the government gave you all the money and food you wanted every day, would you feel like working?"

"No, I'd be surfing all day!"

"That's exactly what happened to the people on the island to my left. The government gave the people food and money whenever they wanted, even when they didn't work!"

"That sounds great!"

"It sounds great, but listen to what happened next. The more food and money the government gave to people, the less they worked. Pretty soon no one was working on the entire island! Since nobody was working, no one was earning money. Since no one was earning money, no one was paying taxes. And since no one was paying taxes, the government was unable to give people what they wanted for very long. The government ran out of money. It couldn't buy ships to fight pirates, the island was attacked many times, and the people went starving. Izzy, one of the most important rules is rule number four: government's primary responsibility is to protect you, not provide for you."

RULE #4

Government's primary responsibility is to protect, not provide.

RULE #4 IN HISTORY

I am for doing good to the poor, but...I think the best way of doing good to the poor is not making them easy in poverty, but leading or driving them out of it. I observed...that the more public provisions were made for the poor, the less they provided for themselves, and of course became poorer. And, on the contrary, the less was done for them, the more they did for themselves, and became richer.

— Benjamin Franklin, 1766

It is the moral obligation of government to cast a temporary safety net to the drowning citizen. However, the temptation of government to turn safety nets into safety lifestyles is almost too great to withstand, as victims in need become dependable voters. Many have looked to the Nordic model as an example of government welfare that works, but a report from J.P. Morgan provides insight, "Copy the Nordic model if you like, but understand that it entails a lot of capitalism and pro-business policies, a lot of taxation on middle-class spending and wages, minimal reliance on corporate taxation, and plenty of co-pays and deductibles in its health care system."[1]

After seeing his country held up as an example of successful government welfare during an American presidential debate, then-Danish prime minister Lars Løkke Rasmussen told students in a 2015 speech at Harvard's Kennedy School of Government, "I know that some people in the US associate the Nordic model with some sort of socialism. Therefore, I would like to make one thing clear. Denmark is far from a socialist planned economy. Denmark is a market economy."

Perhaps immigrants from the Nordic countries themselves can shed the greatest light. Danish Americans have a 55 percent higher living standard than Danes, Swedish Americans have a 53 percent higher standard than Swedes, and Finnish Americans enjoy a 59 percent increase in living over Finns.[2] Regardless of continent or culture, government-provided benefits tend to result in a decline in motivation to work, an unmanageable sovereign debt, or both.

BREAKING THE RULE: Sweden

The 500 Percent Mortgage

Between 1870 and 1936 Sweden's economic policies were characterized as "free market." Government involvement was minimal, taxes were lower than in the United States, the economy was deregulated, and public spending was below 10 percent of GDP. As a result, Sweden grew more rapidly than any other Western European country.[2] By the 1970s Sweden ranked as the world's fourth wealthiest country, and the people grew very trusting of their politicians, who proposed an experiment that would increase taxes but redistribute most of the wealth. The thought was that there was plenty of money for everyone, it was just currently in the wrong hands. Johan Norberg, a Swedish historian, adds, "We thought we could do anything, and we had all of those other preconditions: the work ethic, some sort of social pressure, which meant that people were doing the right things, and they wouldn't want to live on the dole."[3]

Between 1970 and 1991 Sweden introduced a centralized economic plan with government provided benefits to the entire population. Citizens could expect free public hospital treatment, free maternity clinics for prenatal care, free dental care for children, cash bene-fits for sick days, monthly payments to parents for each child, twelve months' paid leave for each child in their first year in school, and a guaranteed pension in retire-ment. The Swedish welfare state started out as a safety net for the needy, but taxes grew higher and higher as the government provided more and more benefits to the people.

"The problem with these policies is that they began to erode the foundations for a successful society," Norberg says. Reversing Sweden's traditions of small government and an open economy disintegrated its suc-cessful business climate. IKEA founder Ingvar Kamprad, for example, moved to Denmark in 1974. Successful ath-letes like Björn Borg also fled the country.[4] In 1976, Astrid Lindgren, the creator of Pippi Longstocking, received a tax bill for 102 percent.[5] At home, the Swedes started taking advantage of the system instead of keeping up with their usual productivity, as was originally assumed. People would call in sick more often. "It resulted in less work, people preferring to stay at home and paint the house rather than hiring someone to do it, general lack of getting the kind of education that matters."[3]

Sweden fell from being the fourth richest country in the world to the fourteenth. Its very nature as a coun-try had changed. Susanna Hoffman writes in her article about Sweden, "An authoritarian-like government was necessary to ensure the population did not abuse its welfare system."[4] Between 1970 and 1984, the public sector absorbed the entire growth of the Swedish workforce, with the largest number of new jobs created in social services.[6] No private sector jobs were added whatsoever. Public spending as a share of GDP almost doubled and peaked at 67 percent in 1993. Investors panicked and lost all confidence in the Swedish government. Sweden's growth rate fell to the second lowest among Western European countries[2], the country plunged into what was known locally as the "black-of-night crisis," the banking system seized up, and interest rates briefly rose to 500 percent![7]

BREAKING THE RULE: Finland

Guaranteed Income in the Happiest Country in the World

The concept of guaranteed basic income gathered interest from legislators in the United States and Canada in the 1970s, but Finland was the first to experiment with it in 2017. The idea was to test if guaranteed monthly payments to the people would encourage the unemployed to accept new job offers that they probably wouldn't have otherwise considered, to spend time developing more applicable skill sets, or to engage in entrepreneurial activities. Finland's basic income guarantee was being watched closely by other governments who saw the concept as a way to reduce long-term dependence on the state. Acting as a sort of negative income tax, basic income was designed to pay for itself—as the people receiving it would be willing to take more risks and be more productive if they knew a baseline of security existed.

The basic income program paid $690 per month with no conditions. Two thousand unemployed people, ranging in age from twenty-five to fifty-eight, were chosen to participate at random.[8] Recipients could keep any extra income from work without losing their basic stipend. Also, they were not required to report their incomes to the unemployment office, reducing the stress of threatening the welfare benefits they might already be receiving.[9]

Finland's government declared the experiment a failure after sixteen months and terminated the program at the end of 2018. "We can say that during the first year of the experiment, the recipients of a basic income were no better or worse," one researcher said at Finland's Labor Institute for Economic Research. "The Finnish government hoped that universal basic income would increase labor supply and employment, but it did not," commented Christopher Pissarides, a professor of economics at the London School of Economics and a Nobel Prize winner.[10]

Many were disappointed with the conclusion that providing unemployed people with a minimum income did not encourage them to find work, but instead undermined the fiscal integrity of the state. While 70 percent of Finns supported the idea of basic income, surveys showed that number drop to 35 percent when respondents were told that their already-high income taxes would have to increase further in order to cover the cost of the program.[8] In a review of the Finnish experiment, the Organisation for Economic Cooperation and Development indicated that higher taxes would be needed to pay for the scheme and that, if implemented, it would result in significant income redistribution but also increased poverty.[11]

BREAKING THE RULE: Greece

Debt, the God of Government Crisis

Greece is known to be the birthplace of democracy, Western philosophy, political science, and the Olympics. Every year people travel from all over the world to see its stunning ancient architecture. From the early 1950s to the mid-1970s, it enjoyed one of the highest GDP growth rates in the world, second only to Japan.[12] When Greece joined the European Union in 1981, its economy and finances were in good shape, but the situation deteriorated dramatically over the next thirty years as the government turned to generous welfare policies to keep voters happy.[13]

The public benefits Greece was most famous for were its generous payment increases during working years and its guaranteed retirement pensions. Wages of public sector employees automatically rose every year regardless of performance. Retirement was available when someone reached their fifties. Perhaps the most outrageous (and popular) examples of benefits were the "thirteenth and fourteenth" month payments. Every December, Greek workers were given an additional month's pay to help with holiday expenses. They were also given half a month's pay during Easter and another half when they took vacation.[13] One professor at the University of Athens noted that "during the 1980s and the first half of 1990s there have been no explicit poli-cies . . . to develop cost containment . . . in public spend-ing. The overall objective was to ensure equity at the cost of efficiency."[14]

During the early 2000s, public-sector wages dou-bled and debt was of little concern. The Greek govern-ment and the country's major businesses were able to borrow heavily from international money markets with few credit restrictions. Greece showcased its reckless spending further by buying goods from other countries that didn't work—namely two diesel submarines from Germany that the Greek navy failed to launch.[15] Greece spent vastly more than it took in. In 1974 the ratio of those contributing funds for pensions to those receiving them was more than double than what it was in 2006.[14]

After the financial crisis in 2008, it was clear to investors that a default on Greek repayments was a real possibility. Consequently, they began demanding much higher yields on government notes. Greece eventually fell into an economic depression and its debt-to-GDP ratio had skyrocketed from a 28 percent low in 1981 to 180 percent in 2011.[13] In that same year, 111,000 Greek companies went bankrupt.[16] The next year saw record unemployment,[17] and by 2014 an estimated 44 percent of Greeks lived below the poverty line.

After accepting the biggest financial rescue for an independent nation in history, Greece was forced to implement very steep austerity measures in the form of pension cuts and very high income taxes. "Overtaxation has struck the Greek middle class particularly hard," the Hellenic Federation of Enterprises said. "As a result, the most productive members of the working population are obliged to either put up with low salaries, or [leave]." Some five hundred thousand people left the country from 2010 to 2017. George Tzailakis, a thirty-one-year-old law graduate, moved to Switzerland after he got a job offer from a restaurant in Geneva. "When I got the offer, I didn't even think twice," Tzailakis said. "There is not much you can do with a Greek salary. You cannot build a normal life."[18]

As of 2019, Greece's economy is still 24 percent smaller than it was in 2007. According to an Oxford Economics consulting firm, it could take until 2033 for Greece's GDP to recover to its pre-crisis level. Giorgos Fasois is a Greek man who is trying to wait until things get better, but he may never hold a full-time job again. He just does whatever it takes to feed his three children. His family has sold all the jewelry it owned, including wedding rings. They have moved three times during the crisis to reduce their rent and utility bills. "I live like a zombie," Fasois said. "If you pay all the taxes you have to, you might as well put a stone around your neck and drown yourself." He added that his family hasn't been able to afford a vacation in ten years.

BREAKING THE RULES: Kuwait
Black Gold

Nearly a century ago, oil started to flow in Kuwait. Since then, the country has enjoyed a lifestyle of comfort compared to most. It has the world's sixth largest oil reserves and, according to the World Bank, it has the fourth highest income per capita. However, Kuwait is different from the other Arab states. It's the only one that is at least semi-democratic with an elected parliament, and it is considered the "freest" state in the Middle East.

As a result of the money the government makes from oil sales, Kuwait has chosen to create one of the most generous welfare systems in the world. For instance, after the 1982 stock market crash, Kuwait's ruler at the time wrote off hundreds of millions of dollars in personal debt for the country's citizens. He also forgave almost all consumer debt (worth billions) after the 1991 Gulf War.[20] So long as Kuwait sells oil, its wealth affords all its citizens a very comfortable life. All medical services in public hospitals, from routine check-ups to cancer treatment and prescription drugs, are completely free. Utilities and education are also free.[20] Kuwaitis have guaranteed employment. Ninety-five percent of the population chooses to work in the public sector, making the government the largest employer. Wages are not based on performance, and the government cannot legally fire civil servants except for a criminal offense. If citizens wish to work in the private sector, the government pays them a monthly unemployment allowance until they find a job.[21]

However, in 2013 the Kuwaiti Prime Minister stated, "The current welfare state that Kuwaitis are used to is unsustainable." Forecasts showed that if spending continued unchanged, the country would see a budget deficit by 2021.[22] According to the International

Monetary Fund, Kuwait actually ran a deficit five years earlier. Government spending finally exceeded oil revenues. This presented a real problem. In the eyes of the prime minister, no matter how wealthy the government became, budget deficits for a country heavily dependent on one natural resource was a matter of national security.[20] "It is necessary for Kuwaiti society to transform from a consumer of the nation's resources to a producer," he said. Even Kuwait's ruler in 2017 admitted, "Cutting public spending . . . stopping waste and the bleeding of our national resources . . . has become inevitable."[23]

No economic model that provides for the people can outlive the longevity of profitable productivity. Regardless of the wealth produced either by the government or the private sector, free benefits will eventually cost too much. Not only is sovereign solvency threatened, but the people's nature changes as well. "Kuwait's people used to be very hardworking . . . Unfortunately, with the influx of oil wealth this trait has been gradually reduced. Now they all look for a government job where they work only three hours a day or don't work at all—and it has become so widespread that it affected the values of the society," said a veteran liberal politician who served five terms in Kuwait's parliament.[23] Benefits are not inherently bad, but history has proven that lavish welfare curbs a people's enthusiasm for the political and economic reform necessary to preserve the country in the long run.

RULE NUMBER FIVE

"So the more money I earn, the more things I can buy. But what if someone already has a lot of money; can I still earn a lot of money too?"

"Of course! Just because someone else has a lot of money doesn't mean you have to earn less. From all the islands I've seen during the last few hundred years, Izzy, I've noticed that if someone earns a lot of money, it actually helps other people earn more money too!"

"Really? How?"

"Let me give you an example. On the island to my right, people started businesses that made canoes, fishing nets, and coconut ice cream. Some people were rich, others were poor, but everyone was earning something because they made things other islands wanted to buy. Also, the government let the people keep the money they earned so they were motivated to work harder. The island was earning a total of two hundred coins per day selling those three things. Then a man named Micah starting selling seashell necklaces on the island too. He earned ten coins per day.

So before Micah came, the island was earning two hundred coins, but after Micah came, the island was earning 210 coins every day, right?"

"Right. But how did that make other people rich too?"

"Well, at the end of the day, Micah would take five of his coins to buy coconut ice cream from Cohen. So after selling coconut ice cream to Micah, Cohen was now earning five more coins every day too, right?"

"Right."

"Now, how much money is the island really earning every day, Izzy?"

"Um . . . 210 coins with Micah, plus the five extra coins Cohen earned . . . so 215 coins?"

"That's right!"

"Wait, what?! I thought the island was only earning 210 coins after Micah came. Where did the extra five coins come from?"

"You see, Izzy, this is how money works. The more money someone earns, the more money they can spend buying things from other people and then those other people earn more money too! Micah didn't steal other people's money to get rich, he made something that they wanted to buy!"

"OK, I think I get it. What if there are people who aren't able to work? How do they earn money?"

"Surprisingly, when people are allowed to keep their own money instead of giving it to the government, they tend to be generous with those in need. What happened on the island to my left is a whole different story. The government on that island owned all the businesses, kept all the money they earned, and then paid everyone the same based on what they needed only. The people thought this was the best way to make things fair. There would be no poor people and there would be no rich people. Everybody would be equal. But it didn't work out that way.

Since the government paid the people the same no matter how much they produced, no one on the island was motivated to work hard. And since the government kept all the extra money that was earned, the people had no incentive to innovate tools that would have made businesses more successful. Instead of making canoes, they only used logs of wood to float on. Instead of crafting nets to catch more fish at once, they just used spears to kill what they needed to eat day to day. As a result, the island didn't make a lot of things that other islands were willing to buy.

Now because the government owned all the businesses, it was able to force the people to work or they would be punished! But that only made the people work just hard enough to survive. Eventually, the government ran out of money and the people went starving. So here's rule number five, Izzy: businesses must be owned by the people, not the government."

RULE #5

Businesses must be owned by the people, not the government.

RULE #5 IN HISTORY

A wise and frugal government . . . shall restrain men from injuring one another, shall leave them otherwise free to regulate their own pursuits of industry and improvement, and shall not take from the mouth of labor the bread it has earned. This is the sum of good government.

—Thomas Jefferson, 1801

The most predictable characteristic that governs human behavior is self-interest. Adam Smith observed this in *The Wealth of Nations* : "It is not from the benevolence of the butcher, the brewer, or the baker, that we expect our dinner, but from their regard to their own interest. We address ourselves, not to their humanity but to their self-love, and never talk to them of our own necessities but of their advantages." Does mankind do anything if not for the belief that it benefits himself? Therefore, the most efficient governance a political body can ever hope to achieve establishes appropriate boundaries within which the people can work out their own success. The maximum economic output a country can possibly produce is contingent upon the level of financial rewards its individual citizens can expect to keep. Hence they develop a willingness to take risk, to innovate, to develop new technologies, and to produce more efficiently in a free-market economy, all for the hope of receiving greater gains in the future as further value is provided to the whole of society. Progress is incentivized.

Government is not held to such a high standard. Where the people must create value to survive, the government can simply claim it through taxation. Government creates nothing because it doesn't have to! Unfortunately, its power to protect can also be used to confiscate in the name of national development. Instead of applying its proper scope in tandem with the organic pace of economic development, government's tendency is to take a proactive role to speed things up. Political power is easily mistaken as the engine of progress.

Businesses fall under state control, private property is abolished, pricing controls are enforced, and profit is taken away. Incentives are forfeited while production quotas stay the same or even increase. This model always yields worse economic results in the long run. Some believe centralized asset allocation would maximize the country's utilization of its resources. That would be true if only assets could manage themselves without the supervision of a self-interested people.

To ensure the proper use of capital, there is no better institution than that bound to consider profit and loss. The business organization, then, is the ultimate fail-safe against inefficient use of the means of production. Without incentives to perform, the government-controlled industry will immediately see improper allocation of assets, lack of innovation, poor quality, and eventual unproductivity and starvation among the people. American economist Milton Friedman once joked that if you put the government in charge of the Sahara desert, in five years there would be a shortage of sand.

Worse yet, a government in control of everything never blames itself. As the people's self-interest overcomes altruistic nationalism, motivation declines and an impatient politic typically resorts to punishment. Therefore, private ownership is the most effective deterrent against revolt. Strong growth can occur under an authoritarian regime, but the positive results will prove temporary at best. With a disincentivized citizenry, growth will continue only until the country's technology becomes obsolete, its resources are depleted, or until the people revolt against the political system itself. Thus, long-lasting economic progress can only be maintained if it's not impeded by the financial losers of technological advancement, or by the political losers of temporary power.

FOLLOWING THE RULE: Australia

Two Tickets to Paradise

After the 1707 union of England, Wales, and Scotland, Great Britain devised a solution to transport local criminals to overseas colonies throughout the empire. Australia seemed a good alternative after the United States of America declared its independence in 1776. The penal colony of New South Wales was located in the heart of modern-day Sydney and consisted of convicts and their guards.

Thanks to Acemoglu's and Robinson's research, we have a very detailed account of what happened next. Initially the convicts had no rights. They couldn't own anything, they couldn't go to court for injustices, they had to perform forced labor, and the guards intended to keep what the prisoners' produced without paying them for it. Since the convicts were given only food for their work, they had no incentives to perform above what was minimally required. The guards wanted more and thought about exploiting the Aboriginals (local tribes), but in the end they decided it was best to simply let the convicts work and keep their produce for themselves.

Of course, the guards still kept some of the financial gains of the convicts' work, but production increased. Convicts became entrepreneurs who hired other convicts. They were given land, and all their rights were restored once their sentences were over. Having inadvertently established a free market, the guards themselves became very rich by selling rum to the convicts and developing sheep farms. Convicts also grew wealthy. One convict in particular, Henry Kable, became extraordinarily rich. Sent to the penal colony in 1788, Henry eventually owned a hotel, bought a ship to trade sealskins, and owned more than nine farms, multiple homes, and shops all across Sydney by 1809.[1]

FOLLOWING THE RULE: England

A Bloodless Revolution

The Glorious Revolution, also called the Bloodless Revolution, took place in 1688. King James II was replaced by his daughter Mary and her Dutch husband William of Orange on conditions that the power of the monarchy would be limited, giving more authority to an elected parliament. This event marked the beginning of a political democracy in the realm. Only Parliament had the authority to pass laws and impose taxes. The people had the right to petition the king without fear of repercussions, to freely elect representatives to Parliament, and to expect protection of private property.

It is not surprising to see the Industrial Revolution occur shortly thereafter. Innovations could be profitably sold in the market economy. This generated vast financial incentives for inventors with great ideas such as James Watt, who perfected the design of the steam engine to improve power, efficiency, and cost-effectiveness. James Watt wrote to his father: "I have at last got an Act of Parliament vesting the property of my new Fire engines . . . throughout Great Britain and the [American 13 colonies] for twenty five years to come, which I hope will be very beneficial to me, as there is already considerable demand for them."[2]

With financial incentives came technological advances. Isambard Kingdom Brunel was an English mechanical and civil engineer who is now considered one of the most ingenious engineers in history. Brunel built dockyards, bridges, and tunnels. He developed the first propeller-driven steamship to cross the Atlantic and built the first tunnel under a navigable river. Brunel's designs revolutionized public transport and modern engineering in England.

These inventors, among others, were motivated by the market opportunities they anticipated in Great Britain and its colonies overseas. Innovation was now incentivized with private property protection, which included intellectual property and financial gains.

FOLLOWING THE RULE: South Africa

Charity from the Prosperous

One final example from Africa, again, comes from *Why Nations Fail*. European settlers in the nineteenth century were very much attracted to South Africa. It had a temperate climate and was free of diseases, such as malaria and yellow fever, that made West Africa the "White Man's Graveyard." With the discovery of diamond and gold mines in the late 1860s, the British wanted to expand their control. This created significant opportunities for native Africans. There was great demand for agricultural produce and trade, so locals invested heavily in new clothes, ploughs, wagons, irrigation, and other farming technology. A magistrate in the area noted that about eight thousand African farmers had bought and were developing ninety thousand acres of land.

The prosperity of the local farmers was highlighted in a letter from a missionary to England where he said he collected forty-six pounds of cash for the "Lancashire Cotton Relief Fund."[3] The prosperous

African farmers were actually donating money for relief to the poor English textile workers!

BREAKING THE RULE: USSR

From Russia without Love

After a brief civil war, the Russian Empire was reorganized in 1922 as the Union of Soviet Socialist Republics (USSR) under the leadership of Vladimir Lenin. Lenin maintained a near free-market economy to rebuild the Soviet Union from the destruction of World War I and its own civil war. It worked, and production for the country regained its 1913 levels. Following Lenin's death, Joseph Stalin came to power, but Russia was still "behind" the West. Stalin felt the economy wasn't delivering progress fast enough and feared Russia's inability to compete. "We are fifty or a hundred years behind the advanced countries. We must make up this gap in ten years. Either we do it or they will crush us,"[4] he said.

In order to catch up to the West and increase the pace of industrialization, Stalin replaced the market economy with a centrally planned economy. Peasant property and entire villages were absorbed by the government.[5] Within individual business sectors, government planning ministries defined labor and raw material requirements, schedules of completion, and pricing. It is interesting to note that Stalin turned to

Marxist socialism with the belief that it would simply speed up the positive quasi-capitalist effects Lenin employed previously. However, this put the decisions of capital allocation with the state, which usually yields inefficient results compared to business owners who are incentivized by profit. Investments that serve political agendas tend to regard cost as a second thought compared to the government's vision of what "could be" if only more is contributed.

Resources were diverted from all over the country to accomplish very specific goals, including heavy manufacturing, consumer goods, and military armaments. The goal was to transform the Soviet Union from an agricultural state into an industrial powerhouse. Stalin initiated his plan in 1928, describing it as a "new revolution from above."[6] It is not uncommon for those with government power to assign divine inspiration to their political initiatives, making it easier to ostracize those most likely to disagree. Stalin eliminated academic institutions, literary journals, publishing houses, and theatres.[7] He also arrested tens of thousands of teachers and intellectuals.[8]

The engine of the USSR's industrialization was agriculture. Stalin established collective farming systems that forced hundreds of thousands of peasants to labor for the state. The wealthy, land-owning farmers were "to be liquidated as a class."[9] The middle and lower class supported collectivization because it took private land and distributed it among the poorer villages.[10] Many landowners still resisted by killing their farm animals rather than turning them over to the government.[11] Farms were assigned mandatory levels of production, but public machine and tractor stations were provided so the peasants could farm the land more effectively.

The number of factory workers doubled from three to six million in just three years.[12] Most of what agriculture produced was sent to feed the ever-growing industrial population.[13] Stalin explained his philosophy in this way: "There is no powerful national movement without the peasant army . . . in essence, the national question is a peasant question."[8] Here, the communist leader admits his policies wouldn't work without a large majority of peasants providing for the state. The danger of working on behalf of the common good is also highlighted: governments that enforce such ideals eventually reap more benefits than the people themselves.

The results of Stalin's economy were initially very promising. Industrial output increased by 50 percent.[14] However, the situation in rural USSR was devastating. Political leaders had mandated unrealistic farm production to fuel the increase. Quotas reached over 200 percent of normal capacity, and farmers just couldn't deliver.[15] As punishment when production targets were missed, armed soldiers were sent to confiscate what little food the peasants had gathered.[8] The rural population began to starve. Peasants killed and ate pets and consumed flowers, leaves, tree bark, and roots. One woman who found some dried beans was so hungry that she ate them on the spot without cooking them and reportedly died when they expanded in her stomach. Two boys who were caught hiding fish and frogs they'd caught were beaten and then dragged into a field with their hands tied and mouths gagged, left to suffocate.[16] In Ukraine, the Great Famine of 1932–33 is estimated to have killed up to ten million people, including up to a third of the nation's children.[8] Alex de Waal, British researcher and executive director of the World Peace Foundation at Tufts University, said, "The Ukrainian famine was a clear case of a man-made famine . . . a hybrid . . . caused by calamitous social-economic policies."[17] Even Mikhail Gorbachev, leader of the Soviet Union from 1985 to 1991, experienced the Soviet famine recalling that "in that terrible year [in 1933] nearly half the population of my native village, Privolnoye, starved to death, including two sisters and one brother of my father."[18]

Government control of resources proved quite inefficient in the long run. Extreme amounts of resources were put into numerous construction projects that were never completed and equipment that was never used.[19] In 1932 grain production was 32 percent below average.[20] Stalin soon realized that to work hard, people needed personal monetary rewards they could keep for themselves rather than simply laboring for the collective good of the country. He introduced a bonus system based on achieving production goals. But the problem with his communist economy was that the prices of goods were still controlled by the government, not determined by the free-market forces of supply and demand. This eliminated any motivation for the people to innovate or to maintain quality. Thus, when bonuses from the government were paid based on the tonnage of sheet metal produced or the cumulative weight of chandeliers manufactured, the people made them extra heavy.[21]

In the end, Stalin enacted laws against absenteeism and idling on the job. Between 1940 and 1955, thirty-six million people had been found guilty of being too lazy. Fifteen million had been sent to prison and 250,000 had been shot.[22] Coercion achieved production goals but not good ideas, which forced the Soviet government to pirate Western computer technology (the IBM 360 platform) because engineering efforts on its own had failed.

Despite the abuses committed by the Soviet government, its national income grew 6 percent per year until 1960.[23] Nobel Prize—winning American economist Paul Samuelson even predicted that national income in the Soviet Union would overtake that of the United States. Though unable to exploit its people forever, Russia still remained relatively rich due to its vast supply of oil and natural gas, but oil prices collapsed in 1986. By 1990 the communist party had crumbled and the Soviet Union's GDP per capita was less than half that of the US.

BREAKING THE RULE: Venezuela

From Riches to Rags

In 1928 Venezuela became the world's second biggest petroleum exporter, and by the 1970s it was the richest country in Latin America, with one of the most stable democracies.[24] However, with the nation's oil revenues going straight to the politicians in power and their cronies, the people became disenchanted. Hugo Chávez ran for president in 1998 and won with a populist message of returning power to the people.

Though his intentions to obliterate poverty might have been sincere, the Chávez government's ownership of the country's most valuable resource provided so much money and power that the temptation to nationalize additional sectors of the economy was too hard to resist. Wealth redistribution via industry confiscation became the business model of preference to provide for the poor. It is estimated that Chávez seized control of six million hectares of agricultural land,[26] saying, "the land is not private. It is the property of the state."[27] Numerous supermarkets were requisitioned from their owners.[25] In 2008 alone, Chávez nationalized the cement industry, Venezuela's largest telephone and electric utilities, and the country's leading steel company.[28,29,30] Then, in 2009 the government seized control of all the rice-processing plants in the country and used the military to force them to produce at full capacity.[31]

Venezuela did see significant improvements during Chávez's presidency. The poverty and infant mortality rates both fell while GDP expanded.[32, 33, 34] However, abuse of power and corruption were rampant. If any business or political elites objected to executive decrees, Chávez would declare them enemies of the state. Licenses of those who expressed criticism in the media were suspended. When labor unions protested, they were replaced. When courts challenged Chávez, he packed them with loyalists. He opposed open markets, liberalized prices, deregulation, property rights, and competition. In 2011 when $500 million from the state-owned oil company's pension fund found its way into a pyramid scheme, none faced prosecution. Perhaps worst of all, Chávez hired political enforcers to disperse protesters. Paid and given arms by the government, they expelled the police force in the nation's capital of Caracas in 2005.[35] "He was reducing potential checks on his authority," says John Carey, associate dean of social sciences at Dartmouth College. "Beneath the revolution-ary language was pretty savvy institutional engineering."

Productivity and quality plummeted. Since gov-ernment produces nothing by itself, any assets it requisitions typically operate less inefficiently. Hence the fallacy of politicians thinking they can do a better job with businesses than the entrepreneurs who created them. Chávez fired eighteen thousand skilled technicians and managers from the state-owned oil company and replaced them with one hundred thousand of his own supporters. Daily production fell by more than one million barrels despite a global boom in oil prices.[36] The injury rate tripled[35] and it was widely suspected that oil revenues were being diverted away from maintenance budgets to the various social programs Chávez pursued.[35] As of 2009, what was once productive farmland is now idle under government hands. Referring to the government officials overseeing the land redistribution, one farmer stated, "These people know nothing about agriculture."[27] After the government nationalized the port at Puerto Cabello, more than 120,000 tons of food sat rotting at the port.[37] Regarding the businesses Chávez seized control over, cement production dropped 60 percent,[38] Venezuela's electrical grid saw frequent blackouts,[39] and steel production declined every year.[40] Today, Venezuela is in dire straits. The number of Venezuelans living in poverty has doubled since 2014. Almost nine out of ten don't have enough money to cover their nutritional needs, and a recent survey showed that more than eight million Venezuelans don't get enough to eat.[41] Many survive by scavenging through garbage piles for leftovers, collecting firewood, gathering wild fruit, and fetching water in streams.[42] Oil production is less than a third of what it was when Chávez came to power in 1999, even though Venezuela sits on top of the largest oil reserves in the world.[26] The murder rate in Caracas has exploded. Public services have collapsed. Bridges and roads are in disrepair, and untreated sewage pollutes drinking water. "It's really hard to think of a human tragedy of this scale outside civil war," said Kenneth Rogoff, an economics professor at Harvard University and former chief economist at the International Monetary Fund. "This will be a touchstone of disastrous policies for decades to come." One can only imagine the economic growth Venezuela might have seen had businesses stayed in the hands of their owners.

BREAKING THE RULE: China
The Great Leap Backwards

After surviving an invasion from Japan and its own civil war, China was in disarray. Machinery in major industrial areas was dismantled. Transportation, communication, and power systems had been destroyed, and food production was low. China used this devastation to engender political zeal. In 1949 the Chinese Communist Party, led by Mao Zedong, established the People's Republic of China with the primary goal to restore the economy to normal working order. After touring the country, Mao believed the Chinese people were capable of anything, especially serving the new government in the name of achieving national goals, it would seem.

Owners of private firms were convinced to sell their businesses to the state or convert them to joint public-private enterprises under state control. The banking system was nationalized. Wealthier farmers were forced to redistribute their property to the 60 percent of farm families that previously owned little or no land at all and then were encouraged to cooperate in agricultural production in teams with several households each. By 1952 commerce had been restored. Industry and agriculture had regained their previous levels of production and actually improved in the succeeding five years.

Like the USSR, China's goals included industrial development. Mao believed the best way to finance industrialization was to establish a monopoly over grain distribution, thus allowing the state to produce at a very low expense (using the limitless supply of cheap labor from peasants) while selling their produce at a much higher price abroad. In 1958 the People's Republic of China initiated the "Great Leap Forward." Households all over China were forced into state-operated communes. Wages were replaced by work points to be redeemed in exchange for food. Mao insisted that farmers maximize their grain production to pay for the construction of offices, factories, and schools and to establish a welfare system for those living in major cities.[43] In the countryside all religious institutions and ceremonies were prohibited, being replaced with political meetings and propaganda sessions.

Mao wanted China to surpass England's industrial output within fifteen years. In the first three years of the Great Leap Forward, thousands of state projects had been started.[44] Because of this industrial investment, the number of Chinese workers employed by the state doubled[45] and grain production became severely strained. As is typical with self-aggrandized authoritative regimes who own the means of production, political agendas hold priority over common sense and the intellectual authority that threatens them. The state knows best, they believe. This sentiment was confessed by Mao himself in later years, when he said, "What's so unusual about Emperor Shih Huang of the China Dynasty? He had buried alive 460 scholars only, but we have buried alive 46,000 scholars."[46]

To raise more capital, Mao tried to increase farm production with untested practices. Policies included close cropping (where seeds are sown far more densely than normal, with the belief this would improve crop yields) and deep plowing (where seeds are sown far more deeply in the soil than usual, with the belief the plants would yield extra-large root systems).[47] Grain production actually decreased.[48] Irrigation and water-control works—built without input from engineers—claimed the lives of hundreds of thousands of exhausted villagers.[49] Though Mao had no personal knowledge of metallurgy, he "encouraged" steel furnaces to be built at every commune. Trees were chopped down and wood taken from the doors and furniture of peasants' homes to fuel the furnaces. Pots, pans, and other metal artifacts were requisitioned by the state to be melted down so Mao's steel targets could be met, but the output was of negligible economic worth. During Mao's push for rapid expansion, coordination suffered and material shortages were frequent.

Despite these setbacks, industrial output did "leap" by 55 percent in 1958. However, in the three years that followed, China experienced the most devastating famine and mass starvation the world has ever seen. The Great Famine has since been characterized as man-made, equivalent to losing the entire population of California, and a direct result of political policy. First, it must be noted that villagers were deprived by Mao's communist party of being able to rent, sell, or use their land as collateral for loans.[43] With no property to their names and no hope to grow their personal wealth, the people lacked all incentives to work efficiently. Dutch historian Frank Dikötter writes in *Mao's Great Famine*, "As incentives to work were removed, coercion and violence were used instead to compel famished farmers to perform labor on poorly planned irrigation projects while fields were neglected."[50]

Meanwhile, the pressure to satisfy Mao was so great that local leaders falsely reported higher grain production results. Some estimate that these figures were inflated as much as ten times the actual amount.[51] As a result, very little grain was left for peasants to eat, since most of it was shipped to major cities to be sold. In fact, those provinces that adopted Mao's reforms with the most vigor suffered the greatest. Sichuan, a province known as "Heaven's Granary" because of its fertility, is thought to have suffered the greatest absolute numbers of deaths from starvation.[52]

The horror of the Great Leap Forward is hard to imagine. People were severely beaten or killed for reporting the real harvest numbers, for refusing to hand over what little food they'd saved for themselves, or for trying to flee the area.[53] Frank Dikötter, again, provides further details: "As mass starvation set in, ever greater violence had to be inflicted in order to coerce malnourished people to labor in the fields. Victims were buried alive, thrown bound into ponds, stripped naked and forced to labor in the middle of winter, doused in boiling water, forced to ingest excrement and urine, and subjected to mutilation."[54]

Author Yan Lianke, who survived the Great Leap Forward, was taught by his mother to "recognize the most edible kinds of bark and clay. When all the trees had been stripped and there was no more clay, he learned that lumps of coal could appease the devil in his stomach, at least for a little while."[55] One story tells of a man who had one of his ears chopped off and his legs tied up with iron wire while his back was branded with a sizzling tool simply for digging up a potato. People accused of not working hard enough were often hung.[56] The agricultural policies of the Great Leap Forward continued until 1961, and latest estimates put the death toll at around forty-five million.[57]

Once Mao's policies were finally abandoned, more people had died than under Hitler and Stalin combined. Though these results may not have been the original intent, they were the natural consequence of a one-party political system whose unbridled power first derived from the confiscation of private property and government control of business. Dali Yang, professor of political science at the University of Chicago concluded, "The best way to prevent the country from following another movement like the Great Leap Forward is to create mechanisms that check those in power."[58]

RULE NUMBER SIX

"You've told me a lot of things, Tommy! I'm not sure I'll be able to remember everything."

"I know what you mean, Izzy. It took me two hundred years to come up with these rules! If I had to give you only one rule more, it would be rule number six: everyone deserves equal treatment under the law, not equal results regardless of how you work."

"What does that mean? Is the government going to help me make coconut ice cream like Cohen does so I can make money too?"

"Actually, Izzy, the government doesn't help you with your business at all. It just makes sure you're not treated unjustly by anyone else. Here's what I mean: to start a coconut ice cream business, first you need to go to the store to buy coconuts, ice, milk, and anything else you need, right?

"Right."

"But what if the store wouldn't sell those things to you because you're a girl, or because you have blonde hair. Is that fair?"

"Of course not!" Izzy said.

"I agree! You should be treated based on your abilities rather than how you look. Everyone deserves the same treatment, and that's what I mean by equal opportunity. It's government's job to make sure everyone on the island treats each other with decency."

"So, it doesn't mean I'll have the same amount of money as Cohen?"

"Not necessarily. Do you remember rule number five, Izzy?"

"Um . . . that government shouldn't own businesses, right?"

"That's right! Remember, if government tries to own businesses, the people won't earn as much than if they had owned the businesses themselves. And since every business sells something different, the amount of money each person earns will be different too. The island to my right had rich people and poor people. It wasn't a perfect system, but it was the best way I've seen for the most number of people to earn the most amount of money. It's up to you, Izzy, to choose which business you'd like to work in."

Tommy continued, "As always, the island to my left did something different. They thought "equal opportunity" meant that it was government's job to get involved with business and to create opportunities for people who weren't as successful as they had hoped. Remember Micah who sold sea shell necklaces?"

"Yes."

"Before living on the island to my right, he lived on the island to my left. He sold necklaces and earned money there. Another man named Karl sold necklaces too, but he didn't earn as much money as Micah. Since the island didn't like that Micah was rich and Karl was poor, the government gave Karl extra help. It helped him make better necklaces and paid other people to buy them at a cheaper price than what Micah was selling his for! Eventually, no one bought necklaces from Micah anymore. Micah ran out of money and he had to move to the island on the right to start over. By trying to make things equal for Karl, the government accidently hurt Micah's business. Izzy, the best way to be fair is to make sure everyone has the same chance to choose how they want work, not to have the same amount of money. Do you understand the difference?"

"I think so."

"Everyone deserves equal treatment under the law while they try to earn money, not equal money regardless of how they work."

"OK, now it makes sense. I think it's time to take me for a ride on your shell!"

"You're right! Hop on, let's see how many waves we can ride before sundown!"

RULE # 6

Government must guarantee equal opportunity, not equal results.

RULE #6 IN HISTORY

The worst form of inequality is to try to make unequal things equal.

—Aristotle

All of us do not have equal talent, but all of us should have an equal opportunity to develop those talents.—

John F. Kennedy

"There are two ways that inequality can be reduced. The rich can be made poorer or the poor can be made richer," observed Professor Edward Lazear at Stanford University's Graduate School of Business. In political vernacular, this dichotomy is best represented by economies that are either centrally planned or driven by free markets. Perhaps the difference in both philosophies can be best explained in terms of scarcity.

Proponents of a centrally planned economy view money and wealth as a finite resource, thus redistribution is justified to achieve equality because others have too much. An extreme parody for this train of thought would be forcing parents to breathe more slowly so their children can have more air. The mistake is to assume that no matter the level of redistribution, people will continue to work at their maximum ability. Self-interest is the greatest determinant of productivity, but without the incentive to keep the gains of your own labor, such policies result in what Winston Churchill described as "the equal sharing of misery." The capacity of production is unmet, while personal effort matches only the minimum requirement to survive.Fortunately, society doesn't live in a vacuum. Free market enthusiasts welcome as many people to breathe as heavily as they want! Money is not viewed as a resource at all but as a byproduct of serving the needs of others—which are never-ending. Therefore, redistribution of wealth is not necessary because the amount of money is limitless since everyone will always have problems to solve, and the availability of money is widespread since anyone can choose to solve them. So long as the possibility of profit exists, self-interest benefits the common good.

Ultimately, the choice to be made is equal poverty or unequal prosperity. History sheds a more positive light on the unequal prosperity of free markets. Those who implement them have seen a substantial increase in income for the greatest number of their citizens. Additionally, Professor Lazear cautions against turning to government: "There is no compelling evidence that the poorest citizens of rich countries fare better when there is more government control of the economy."[1] Still, there are many who believe a hybrid structure of aggressive government spending within a free market could achieve the best of both worlds. This comes at a severe cost. Data from countries around the world suggests that when government spending increases just 10 percent of GDP, the economic growth rate declines up to 1 percent in response.[2] In America, for example, a drop of 1 percent in growth would mean a total loss of income equal to $354,000 per person over thirty years![2]

Within free-market economies, the bandage to inequality usually takes the form of subsidies and regulation, which often expedites the poor economic prognosis instead of curing it. Here are a few examples: Following the premise of equal pay regardless of job function, San Francisco raised its minimum wage in 2003. However, reports in 2016 found that restaurants have since raised meal prices by 52 percent and 18 percent fewer servers have been hired.[3] By raising the minimum wage, the government made it more expensive for restaurants to hire servers who rely on tips. Subsidized loans have increased the availability of credit for students, but a recent study found that tuition increases sixty cents for every dollar the government makes available to lend.[4] By helping more students pay for college, the government incentivized universities to increase costs. In an effort to reduce consumer banking fees, the US government limited charges that debit card merchants could impose per swipe. However, a report in 2019 found that banks recouped their lost revenue by increasing monthly fees by 70 percent on checking accounts instead, and the number of low-income bank customers who could no longer afford the monthly fee actually increased by one million.[5]

Aside from often yielding the opposite of the intended effect, government involvement in business undermines its primary responsibility to enforce the law equally. The door to corruption opens wide when a political entity tasked with making laws chooses individual recipients for its financial aid. As Cuba found out when Soviet aid stopped coming with the collapse of the USSR, what government can dole out can be taken away. Better to employ the safeguard of not giving politicians the option to provide in the first place.

Indeed, the staples of a free-market economy are equality of opportunity for the people to work out their own prosperity and the rise of personal income that naturally follows. Perhaps the most poignant examples are those countries that were once centrally planned or under totalitarian rule, but then who enacted free-market reforms to improve their economic condition.

FOLLOWING THE RULE: Sweden

Back in the Saddle

As a member of the Swedish parliament, Johnny Munkhammar gave lectures all over Europe about economic reform. He was often asked, "But you come from Sweden, which is socialist and successful—why should we launch free-market policies?" His response clarifies a common misconception. Sweden's modern economic history has been predominately capitalist and "[its] socialism lasted only for a couple of decades, roughly during the 1970s and 1980s."[6] During those two decades, Sweden became a welfare state. The government owned much of the country's resources and determined pricing. Successful businesses were taxed heavily, while those that were inefficient or failing were subsidized. Sweden's laws prohibited wages from being cut and restricted firing and layoffs.[7] Pensions were guaranteed by the state, and tax laws discouraged investment.

In 1968 Sweden was the world's third-richest country.[8] By 1993, it's ranking had fallen to seventeenth.[2] Unemployment rose sharply, inflation soared, financial crisis ensued, and over twenty years, real wages had increased by only 1 percent.[6] Researchers concluded that Sweden's decline in growth and income was a direct result of the increase in its size of government.[2] By the mid-1990s, national debt had ballooned to 80 percent of GDP.

How did Sweden change course to become the richest of the major European Union countries again as of 2019?[9]

In 1991 a pro-market government came to power and enacted far-reaching reforms that encouraged entrepreneurship and rewarded a stronger work ethic. For-profit schooling was introduced along with free school choice nationwide. Parts of the healthcare system were privatized, while the welfare system was converted from a "defined benefits" plan to a "defined contribution" plan. Personal pension accounts are managed by private fund managers and adjust their payouts per contribution levels and market performance. Sweden's pension system is now the most privatized in all of Europe.[7] Government ministries that propose new spending plans are required to submit offset budget cuts for other areas along with them.[9] Unemployment benefits and paid sick leave have been reduced. Most of Sweden's economy is now deregulated, as state-owned companies have been sold off to private investors. Between 1993 and 2000, social spending dropped 24 percent and subsidies were reduced by 80 percent! Finally, taxes have gone down. Corporate taxes have been cut from 57 percent to 22 percent, while wealth and estate taxes have been abolished.[10]

Sweden still employs strong social policies like most of Europe, but the country has instilled a fiscally conservative, free-market infrastructure to sustain it. After all, a country can choose for itself what to spend its surplus money on. Still, as a result of these radical changes, Sweden's national debt has decreased 48 percent from the 1990s, and the country now ranks sixth in the world for protecting private property.[7] From 1991 to 2014, Sweden experienced the second highest growth rate in Western Europe and, most important, real wages increased by 35 percent. Businesses have become more productive and living standards have improved. Munkhammar observed of the "new" Sweden, "More people eat at restaurants now, more people travel abroad, more people buy DVDs and new cars. More people get more."[6]

FOLLOWING THE RULE: China

A Change in Fortune

From 1950 to 1973, the Chinese economy was centrally planned, with the state owning all the natural resources and businesses. GDP per capita grew 2.9 percent per year on average, but party leaders concluded that Maoist policies had failed to produce sufficient economic growth. They also caused China to fall behind the industrial nations of the West, including those in Asia. While Japan competed against European countries in modern technology, China's citizens had to worry about sufficient food supplies, rationed clothing, and inadequate housing. By the late 1970s, food production had become so low that government officials began warning the people of famine, the kind that had killed millions before. 84 percent of China's population lived on less than $1.25 per day. However, by 2011 that percentage dropped below 6 percent.[1]

What did China do to increase the standard of living for 78 percent of its population?

Deng Xiaoping became China's de facto leader in 1978, with clear reforms in mind to advance the country's economy. Deng's focus was not to abandon communism and the government planning that came with it, but to make it work better by allowing free-market mechanisms to take a larger role in the system. "We mustn't fear to adopt the advanced management methods applied in capitalist countries," he said.[11]

What's interesting is that farmers had undertaken changes at the local level already. Until then, people were forced to convert their land into communes, private property had been extinguished, and families were required to produce crops for the state. But in November 1978, desperate villagers gathered at night to sign a pledge that divided the commune's land back into family plots again. They all agreed to deliver the required quota of corn to the government, but then they would keep any surplus for themselves. "In the case of failure," the pledge stated, "we are prepared for death or prison." The next spring the village reported a harvest that equaled their total output between 1955 and 1970 combined![12]

To his credit, Deng urged the communist party to "seek truth from facts." When news reached Beijing of dissenting farmers who were actually growing more food, Deng abolished the collective farming policy and initiated the country's most popular reform: the household contract responsibility system. Peasants were now allowed to work plots of land for profit as long as they also sold a contracted portion of their crops to the state.[13] Whatever food they grew beyond the government quota could be sold in the free market at unregulated prices. This arrangement created strong incentives for farmers to increase productivity. Annual family incomes quickly rose by a factor of twenty.[12] The son of one of the original farmers who signed the pledge elaborated on why his father risked death for economic freedom: "My father signed that paper because we were starving . . . In the end, that's just our human instinct."[12] Nothing is more effective than the profit motive to spur high performance. Between 1975 and 1985 agricultural production increased by 25 percent, justifying the privatization of other parts of the economy.[13]

At about the same time, Deng also announced the Open Door policy, which catapulted China toward becoming the "World's Factory." In order to modernize China's industry, foreign companies had to feel welcome to establish businesses there. Deng created a handful of special economic zones (SEZs) that were relatively free of the government interventions and burdensome taxes that had dampened economic growth elsewhere. An internal communist document revealed the rationale for the SEZs: "Just as our leader Deng has said, the SEZ is a window for observing contemporary capitalism."[14]

Almost immediately Boeing started selling aircraft to Chinese airlines and Coca Cola expressed interest in building a production plant in Shanghai. Shenzhen was the first economic zone to be established, and it showed the most rapid growth, averaging 40 percent per year between 1981 and 1993.[15]

Though much progress resulted from the reforms above, most of China's industry remained state-owned. That changed in 1986. Private ownership through company shares was recognized, creditor rights for repayment of debts were protected, and intellectual property through patents were defined.[1] China's government slowly acknowledged the importance of the private sector. Even after Deng's death in 1997, his handpicked successors continued large-scale privatization. All but a few state enterprises were sold to private investors. In just four years the number of state-owned businesses decreased by 48 percent.[16] With a larger private sector came greater overall economic growth. By 2005 private business accounted for as much as 70 percent of the country's GDP[17] and China surpassed Japan as the largest economy in Asia. From multiple estimates, China's economy experienced an unprecedented average annual growth rate of 9.5 percent between 1978 and 2012.

It would be hard to find a more stark difference in economic growth and its direct correlation to political policy than what China saw under Mao compared to Deng. Deng was by no means perfect. Belonging to the communist party, his regime still committed several human rights abuses. However, the prosperity that grew from his initiatives cannot be denied. The entrepreneurial attitude of the Chinese people saved the country from ruin. In 2018, World Bank president Jim Yong

Kim noted, "China has increased its per capita income 25-fold and more than 800 million Chinese people lifted themselves out of poverty as a result."[18]

FOLLOWING THE RULE: The United States of America

Land of the Free

During the eighteenth century, European nations operated a mercantile economic system. Central governments would settle colonies around the world and treat them as localized business ventures. The colonies would farm and mine raw materials that would then be exported as a financial surplus back to the "parent" country. The same arrangement existed between Britain and her thirteen American outposts, which produced and exported goods including tobacco, dried fish, and lumber back to the Empire. In 1770 the economic output of the thirteen colonies made up 40 percent of the GDP of Britain.[19] However, within six years America declared its independence and about a century later it had replaced Britain as the world's leading economy with an income per capita that was 26% higher.[20]

Countries that have existed much longer than the United States have only dreamed of such rapid prosperity. China and the USSR tried aggressive expansion but at great human cost and misery. What did America do different?

Instead of continuing to treat the people as extensions that served the Crown, the US government empowered American settlers to benefit themselves. Economist Adam Smith argued in *The Wealth of* Nations that the pursuit of self-interest actually helps the nation as a whole if it is constrained by law and morality. No other country has embraced this philosophy more. The US constitution turned the country into a free market. Citizens had property rights, and there was no income tax. The government then passed the Patent Act, which gave exclusive commercial rights to inventors for fourteen years. This incentivized people to take risks and to develop better technologies because they could keep the wealth they generated. During the late 1800s alone, the US Patent Office issued half a million patents for inventions; more than ten times as many as were issued in the previous seventy years and far more than in any other country during the same time.[21] Oliver Evans, as an example, created the high-pressure steam engine which revolutionized the transportation industry from steam boats to railroads.

Alan Greenspan and Adrian Wooldridge recount the progress America saw during this time in their book *Capitalism in America*:

In the decades between the end of the Civil War and the outbreak of World War I, the United States became a recognizably modern society. In 1864, the country still bore traces of the old world of subsistence. Cities contained as many animals as people, not just horses but also cows, pigs, and chickens . . . By 1914, Americans drank Coca-Cola, drove Fords, rode underground trains, worked in skyscrapers . . . shaved with Gillette's disposable razors, lit and heated their houses with electricity, flew in airplanes . . . and gabbed on the phone, courtesy of AT&T.[22]

Indeed, when a people is left alone to work out their own financial future, they will rise to the occasion. Today, the US is the most powerful economy in the world, with the highest standard of living for its middle class. America has the highest average household and employee income among developed countries,[23] the US dollar is the world's foremost reserve currency, the nation has one of the highest net migration rates, it has the world's largest consumer market, and it houses the largest number of billionaires.[24] Foreign direct investments run into the trillions of dollars, and America's economy is at the forefront of technological innovation and energy production.

PART II

GOVERNMENT VS. BUSINESS: THE TWO "ISLANDS" IN AMERICA

AMERICA'S EARLY DAYS

•••••••••••

In the early 1600s the North American continent was largely unknown to the rest of the world. Alan
Greenspan and Adrian Wooldridge observed in their
book *Capitalism in America* that the continent was mainly
inhabited by local Indians and produced less wealth
than even the smallest European city. Today, the United
States of America is the world's biggest economy with
the highest standard of living for the middle class.

How did thirteen colonies grow into the most prosperous country in history and what role did government
play to make this happen?

History is filled with examples of people forced to
gather natural resources throughout the country, only
for their governments to choose how to best use them
to achieve progress. China's communist party hoarded
the entire nation's grain supply to fund its industrialization. Venezuela's regimes controlled all of the country's oil to pay for its numerous social programs. Great
Britain confiscated goods from its overseas colonies
to finance its expanding Empire. Countless others had

simply resorted to high taxes and business nationalization. What made America different was that the people themselves were treated as the most valuable resource. Its infant government played the role of a silent partner only, stepping in to solve larger macroeconomic problems, while the people worked out their own individual success.

The role of government in the United States was to create confidence for the economy to grow naturally. It began by providing land for commercial development. The country's size doubled with the Louisiana Purchase from Napoleon Bonaparte, but the government didn't keep the land. It gifted land away to citizens and businesses! Through the Homestead Act, settlers were offered 160 acres if they worked the land for at least five years. Congress gave away parcels to the railroads to lay track that connected the homesteaders to the established economy in the east.

Now that materials from one end of the country could be delivered to New York and then shipped to Europe on a predictable schedule, America inserted itself into the global economy fairly quickly.

Later on, the government attracted skilled immigrants to fill the growing need for manufacturing. After all, a nation's wealth is solely dependent on a population that can generate it. Congress passed the Act to Encourage Immigration, which allocated federal money to recruit foreign workers. With property rights already in place, it was the people that brought about the Industrial Revolution and demonstrated that inventing something from scratch was not a prerequisite to wealth. The most well-known titans of industry simply excelled at organizing technologies that already existed. Sir Henry Bessemer from Britain discovered how to generate high-quality steel, but Andrew Carnegie created better results that supplied the demand for locomotives, pipelines, bridges, and skyscrapers. Edwin Drake struck oil in Pennsylvania, but it was John Rockefeller who started his own oil-barrel factory and built pipelines that connected oil fields with refineries. The internal combustion engine was developed in Germany, but Henry Ford was the one who created the assembly line to mass produce the Model T for "the great multitude." By 1920 immigrants accounted for more than half of all manufacturing workers in the United States, and America's population multiplied by a factor of fifteen.[1]

For 138 years since its founding, America maintained a relatively consistent track record of free market policy. Predictable politics bred business optimism. Greenspan and Wooldridge noted that many believed the titans of the industrial revolution made themselves rich at the expense of the rest of the population. It must be remembered, though, that the rest of the population enjoyed an affordable higher standard of living because those industrial geniuses exploited economies of scale, not price gouging. The price of steel had already fallen 72 percent during the late 1800s,[2] and by the 1920s, the price of oil declined from sixteen dollars per barrel to around one dollar,[2] Ford reduced the price of his cars from $950 to $269,[3] and the cost of electricity dropped 6 percent per year for over twenty years straight.[4]

The US government proved to be a valuable partner in the early days of the republic. In 1810 there were only two cities with populations more than fifty thousand. By the start of the Civil War, there were sixteen.[5] America had more miles of railroad than the United Kingdom, France, and Germany combined.[6] Everyone seemed to belong to what French diplomat Alexis de Tocqueville called the "cult of the entrepreneur."

A SHIFT IN ATTITUDE

•••••••••••

In 1887 President Grover Cleveland vetoed a bill to provide seed-grain funding for Texas farmers devastated by a drought. He is quoted as saying, "I do not believe that the power and duty of the general government ought to be extended to the relief of individual suffering which is in no manner properly related to the public service or benefit."

The question must then be asked, At what point should the federal government interfere with private business on behalf of the common good?

Nationalization is government intervention in its most extreme form and was most appropriately demonstrated during World War I with the railroads. European nations had ordered billions of dollars' worth of military supplies from US factories, but the train terminals simply weren't designed to handle such a high volume at once. Thousands of railroad cars just sat idle on the tracks with their cargo. To ensure US allies had the materials they needed to fight the war, President Woodrow Wilson felt he had no choice but to nationalize the railroad industry under the United States Railroad

Administration (USRA). The USRA spent $380 million building new rail cars and locomotives, and it eliminated non-essential train routes. If there ever was a national emergency that warranted nationalization of a private business, it should follow the guidelines of the Railroad Control Act. The act required that the railroads be returned by the government to their owners and that the owners would be compensated for the usage of their property. In just over two years, the railroads became private property again. The government's takeover was temporary by law. It achieved a well-defined, short-term purpose to deliver physical goods in a time of need. Most important, it did not turn privately created assets into a perpetual revenue stream for the state.

Still, many Americans began hoping for a permanent repair to their sense of injustice as a result of the great fortunes successful corporations created for their founders. People wondered why an economy capable of producing so many millionaires was unable to make poverty a thing of the past. Capitalism is the worst economic philosophy, except for every other model the world has tried on a large scale. Of course, America's growth saw corruption, pollution, and threats to safety, but it would be unreasonable to substitute the country's progress for an un-tested system we know is better only in the mind's eye.

Rather, current economic systems should be compared to the next realistic alternative.

As an example, farmers began complaining that their profession was in long-term decline. They were right, but it was not because of sinister corporate manipulation. The productivity improvements brought by tractors meant it took less effort to do more work, and people began moving to the city. This phenomenon was precisely the vehicle that provided more employment opportunities for the public good in new sectors of the economy that were previously non-existent (lawyers, bankers, advertising, etc.). The only realistic alternative was to prohibit technological innovation and maintain the status quo of working from sun-up to sun-down on a farm without creating a higher standard of living. It is likely horse breeders were unhappy with the widespread adoption of Ford's Model T, but overall greater efficiencies and wealth for the common man were accomplished because of it.

Nevertheless, people's anger continued to build and culminated with the legalization of an income tax in 1913 when Woodrow Wilson became president. With Theodore Roosevelt's and Wilson's progressive administrations, many new federal agencies had been created. It is interesting to see the benefit of the doubt at this time shift to government from the free-market principles that had made America the number one economy in the world in the first place. Progressives thought the government deserved a perpetual second chance to prove itself if only it was given more time, more people, and more money to work for it. In 1913 the highest tax rate was 7 percent, but by 1918, it had shot up to 77 percent to help finance US participation in World War I. What's most alarming is that after the war ended the tax rates remained at their war-time levels. Pinpointing the causes of market downturns is extremely difficult. It is not unreasonable to conclude, though, that the recession of 1920, which saw corporate revenues fall by 40 percent and unemployment balloon to 11 percent, could in part be attributed to the twenty-fold increase in government spending and high taxes. Both of which didn't exist at such large proportions less than ten years previous.

The key to proper government is temporary actions that do not turn into permanent expenditures. Government is ungrateful and always hungry. Once an agency, tax, or social program finds its way on the plate, government gluttony is almost impossible to satisfy. Nearly every government program undertaken in the 1930s reflected what had already been put in place twenty years earlier during World War I.[1]

THE ROARING
TWENTIES

• • • • • • • • • • • •

As with other countries, America's political power changes hands. While Theodore Roosevelt and Woodrow Wilson practiced governmental activism, their successors Warren Harding and Calvin Coolidge believed in restraint. Described as "executive do-nothings," these two presidents practiced "active [governmental] inactivism."[1] They believed government should be small and selective with its attention, that the job of the president himself was to provide a stable foundation upon which business could create wealth. Coolidge remarked that, "If the federal government should go out of existence, the common run of people would not detect the difference in the affairs of their daily life for a considerable length of time."[2]

During the 1920s, Harding and Coolidge worked with Congress to reduce tax rates to 24 percent. Estate taxes were cut in half. The Supreme Court ruled against the power of unions[3] and minimum wages.[4] Trade union membership plummeted and the number of strikes fell.[5] As a result, average GDP growth per year was over 5 percent during the 1920s compared to the anemic average of 2 percent during the Roosevelt administration.

In America's case, we can assume that either political party wants what's best for the country. The underlying philosophy of Harding and Coolidge was simply that business was a better engine of social progress than government.

Does the profit-motive engender social progress more effectively than governmental activism?

Because of pro-business policies, the largest companies grew over 6 percent per year.[5] With business owners confident in their ability to consistently make a profit, employees increasingly benefited along with them. From Greenspan and Wooldridge's book we know that George Johnson, a shoe manufacturer, introduced an eight-hour workday and comprehensive medical care. Philip Wrigley made gum but also introduced an income insurance plan and a pension system. Lewis Brown, an asbestos magnate, introduced collective bargaining and conducted regular surveys of employee opinion.[6] By 1929 about 50 percent of all corporate dividends went to people who earned $5,000 a year or less.[7]

Social progress automatically occurs within companies that are optimistic about their financial future. Inherent in every for-profit business lies the goal to earn more profit, of course, which is achieved by providing its skilled employees with incentives to stay. Like capitalism, individual businesses are not perfect. Everyone wishes to be paid more. But the risk of working for a corrupt business under adverse conditions should not justify the forfeiture of an entire system that has created more wealth than any economy in world history—especially when employment alternatives and training for new skill sets exist.

A decent rate of return or a stable wage is the most moral form of wealth distribution. Ironically, society always seems to find ways to skirt compulsory taxes that are meant to achieve the same social goals. During the profitable "Roaring Twenties," the federal debt declined substantially, competition within the monopolistic transportation industry was born, job availability increased, profit-sharing was paid out through dividends, medical coverage was introduced, non-oppressive work schedules were implemented, and long-term wealth distribution through pension plans was offered.

THE GREAT
DEPRESSION

● ● ● ● ● ● ● ● ● ● ● ●

Unfortunately, the Roaring Twenties ended in 1929 with the steepest market crash in US history. Both business and government share the blame. On the one hand, companies made it too easy to purchase everything from clothes to jewelry with borrowed money. Consumer debt had multiplied by a factor of five.[1] On the other hand, government turned extremely protectionist. Anti-immigration policies along with tariffs on hundreds of foreign goods resulted in a 66 percent decline in global trade.[2] Demand for products disappeared and stocks plummeted 89 percent within three years. If there's one thing both business and government have in common, it's the human capital each employ, which naturally results in overreaction and guaranteed volatility. Free markets tend to over-speculate, resulting in the collapse of toxic assets, while governments tend to over-regulate, resulting in the collapse of business confidence.

Though both business and government are needed for optimal growth, which is best suited to spur recovery after downturns occur? No greater contrast of result can be seen than how these two institutions attempted to pull the nation out of the Great Depression's lull. In desperate times, desperate measures seem reasonable—along with the blame that is assigned. Hence, the government's approach to do something, *anything*, but nobody knew exactly what. They just "knew" business was at fault. President Franklin D. Roosevelt declared in a speech in 1932 that "The country needs . . . bold, persistent experimentation."[3]

Government control became an entrepreneurial pursuit. FDR's famous New Deal included a series of new legislation and federal agencies to micromanage the economy. New regulatory codes covered five hundred industries that determined who could produce what and how much they could charge for it.[4] Farmers, in particular, were given subsidies in exchange for fixing their prices and not cultivating their land with the hope of showing strong demand for their produce. Subsidies can be useful, but most likely end with corrupt dependency. Farmers quickly began gaming the system, claiming subsidies for setting aside parts of their farms and then growing the same crops on other pieces of land. William Faulkner quipped, "We no longer farm in Mississippi cotton fields. We farm now in Washington corridors and Congressional committee rooms."[5]

Regardless of political philosophy, everyone can agree the American economy improves when there is strong demand for its products. The government under FDR tried to mimic the results of a robust economy until it reemerged organically. However, the market cannot be fooled with a "fake it until you make it" philosophy. Strong revenues and low inventory are the fruits of high demand, but when accomplished through mandated price-fixing and production limits, the first crucial ingredient of a market recovery is ignored: business confidence.

The capstone of Franklin D. Roosevelt's New Deal was Social Security. He described it as a "pension" that was simply paid back to the people later in retirement for "contributing" payroll taxes now.[6] Money invested for profit in the private sector carried the stigma of greed, but if provided through the government filter, it became a virtue. Some argue that if government provides basic necessities, then the people can focus on being more productive. Hence, they say capitalism creates a waste of latent talents because too much time is spent trying to make ends meet. To that argument the rebuttal must be made that history has never shown the cost of providing basic necessities to the whole of a country's population to be recouped sufficiently by the assumed future innovations of people with more free time. Quite the opposite. Like subsidies, guaranteed income will most likely end with dependency that undermines the need to be productive.

Was the pro-government agenda effective?

By 1937 corporate profits had still plunged and national unemployment was actually higher at 17.2 percent versus 16.3 percent in 1933. FDR's treasury secretary testified in 1939 that "we have tried spending money. We are spending more than we have ever spent before and it does not work . . . I want to see people get a job. I want to see people get enough to eat. We have never made good on our promises . . . I saw after eight years of this Administration we have just as much unemployment as when we started . . . And an enormous debt to boot!"[7]

Why couldn't government reduce employment by itself and grow the economy out of the worst market downturn in US history? The answer lies in its true identity as a governing body, not a producing one. Government is 100 percent dependent on the taxes it extracts from others. It generates no income by itself. Therefore, any steps it takes to stimulate the economy with funding—no matter how great the result—incurs an expense from the people whose money it was originally and which is typically financed through debt. Would anyone take money out of his left pocket just to put it back in his right pocket with an added cost of interest? Yet this is the exact logic behind programs of the state and why treating such as "investments" rarely yields a net positive result.

RECOVERY

●●●●●●●●●●●

America needed to get back to work. Rather than FDR's New Deal, it was World War II that achieved this. War is something no one would wish for. However, it did require an unprecedented volume of production as businesses accepted contracts to manufacture tanks, planes, jeeps, uniforms, tools, food supplies, and more to support Allied troops. The war turned the United States into a manufacturing powerhouse. Major union leaders announced "no strike" pledges. Unemployment disappeared since women and even children had to fill the workforce gap as men left to fight in Europe. Consequently, GDP almost doubled from 1939 to 1944,[1] and America saw its biggest economic boom in history. Half a million new businesses were started and eleven thousand new supermarkets were built.[2]

During this time, government spending increased by a factor of twenty-four to pay for all the war-time supplies. So the question should be asked: If the total amount of money businesses earned from government contracts during WWII was instead distributed to the people, would America have seen the same growth results?

The answer is an emphatic no! When money is earned, someone produces a product and someone buys it. Two parties trade value. Both benefit. However, if money is given, then only the recipient benefits because nothing was produced to earn it in the first place. Herein lies the inefficiency of state-sponsored stimulus. It can only be half as productive as money earned through commerce. Roy Howard, a central figure in American news media and a supporter of FDR, admitted, "There can be no real recovery until the fears of business have been allayed."[3] It is that philosophy that finally made the difference between a prolonged depression and a vibrant economic rebound.

After the war ended and until the early 1970s, the US economy and household income grew every year on average while the top personal tax rates never fell below 70 percent. Some cite these conditions as proof that taxing the rich has a negligible effect on economic expansion and may even help it, but that argument ignores the overwhelming global demand for products that only America was equipped to fill at the time. With the exception of Pearl Harbor, America's manufacturing and delivery infrastructure remained unscathed from WWII, while most of Europe lay in ruins. Global demand supplied by a single country would outweigh the dragging effect of even the highest tax rates. The United States provided 57 percent of the world's steel, 62 percent of the world's oil, and 80 percent of the world's cars.[4] The problem is that such overwhelming demand for only one country to fill may never be seen again. To President Harry Truman's credit after the war, government attempts to control the economy were stifled and business-friendly policies were maintained. "I don't want any experiments," he told his advisor. "The American people have been through a lot of experiments, and they want a rest from experiments."[5]

Did government play a positive role during the extended success of the 1950s and the 60s? Yes.

For one thing, the government won the war. Optimism among the people breeds opportunity in the market. More specifically, Congress passed the GI Bill to provide returning veterans with a wide range of government services to help them move on with life. Of all the government benefits in America, perhaps none are as appropriate as those provided to servicemen willing to sacrifice their own lives for their country. Government invested in technology. The atomic bomb opened doors for private companies to build nuclear reactors for clean energy. Basic research funding at world-class universities and companies initially used to develop new products for the military was also applied to the civilian economy, including medicine. Polio was eradicated from the United States, and 50 percent more drugs were approved by the Federal Drug Administration between 1940 and 1960 than in the fifty years afterward.[6] President Eisenhower's Congress called for forty-one thousand miles of highway to be built. A study of thirty-five industries found that all but three experienced significant cost reductions due to cheaper and more convenient long-distance travel.[7]

It may seem that the more money government invests, the more progress the country will see—technological, economic or otherwise. Is that true?

During the 1950s and '60s America saw exponential public spending, but it followed the recipe for economic success that it used during WWII. Supported by a credible consensus of specific need, public funding went to academic and business entities that had the proven expertise to advance innovation with a high degree of confidence; those innovations could in turn be applied to benefit economic growth. Many still justify increased public funding simply because a budget surplus exists. Though usually met with congratulations, a surplus should be looked upon with extreme skepticism. Since spending cuts are not automatic, government surpluses typically mean the people were just taxed too much. In the end, the goal of the government's income statement should be to break even.

Should government take on investment risk? In principle, risk should be undertaken only by entities with finite resources and the technical know-how to convert them to profitable outputs in a reasonable amount of time. A lemonade stand must sell its drinks quickly enough and for more money than it cost to buy lemons or it will go out of business. Since it can borrow indefinitely and it has no inherent expertise, government can never be as efficient as business. A career politician's technical creativity extends only to campaign promises for the next election year. Without the help from subject matter experts who have usually proven themselves in the private sector first, government can only organize technologies that already exist and thus only see marginal synergies.

THE 1970S: FROM GOLD TO LEAD

•••••••••••

In 1965 the Dow Jones Industrial Average (a stock market index) had climbed to 7,807, but by 1982 it had fallen back down to 2,124, wiping out all the wealth that was created for seventeen years.

What happened?

The clearest transition from the age of growth to the age of decline began during Lyndon B. Johnson's presidency after John F. Kennedy's assassination in 1963. "He adopts [government] programs the way a child eats chocolate chip cookies,"[1] one of Johnson's aides commented. Standing before Congress, Johnson declared an unconditional war on poverty. "The richest nation on earth can afford to win it," he said. "We cannot afford to lose it. We have the opportunity to move not only toward the rich society, and the powerful society, but upward to the Great Society."[2]

Helping those in need is a staple of decent society and must be encouraged, but from whom that help comes and what form it takes yields varying results. Johnson's Great Society relied on federal spending. The government established work programs and educational scholarships; funded transportation, legal, and construction services; subsidized rent for the elderly; and created entitlements that funded medical costs for the poor. While some of Johnson's policies "taught a man how to fish" through work-study and skill-development programs, what remained "gave a man a fish" and assigned massive expansions of costly altruism to electoral-dependent bureaucrats.

Pro-government politicians always seem to possess the best salesmanship, advertising their grand ideas with short, memorable names: Franklin D. Roosevelt's New Deal, John F. Kennedy's New Frontier, and Lyndon B. Johnson's Great Society. Laws based on emotional sound bites are usually passed with the sentiment that the country "can't afford not to do it" and give the government a blank check with no specific metrics to govern its effectiveness. Washington, DC is Disneyland for the active statesman. Oblivious to cost, legislative proposals become rides that deserve experimentation regardless of practicality. With this mind-set, it is no surprise that solving poverty, eliminating hunger and disease, eradicating bad weather, giving away lifetime benefits, legislating equality of outcome, providing free education and healthcare, and any other utopian living condition is considered without pragmatic debate. In just five years the federal deficit totaled more than all previous deficits combined since Johnson took office.[3]

Is it the government's job to provide for her people?

It takes an unwavering entrepreneurial attitude to become president of the most powerful country on earth, but once in office, legislative activism is a slippery slope. "I'm sick of all the people who talk about the things we can't do," Johnson once said. "Hell, we're the richest country in the world, the most powerful. We can do it all."[1]

Fueled by the notion that it is a moral obligation to "do something" with such great power, some politicians and their voters equate government aid with their personal willingness to help others, particularly the poor and the disadvantaged. Hence the belief that the more government provides for its citizens, the more they can justify American exceptionalism and satisfy religious edict.

This mind-set creates a moral dilemma. Federal handouts carry with them the corrupt quid pro quo of partisan votes and debt accumulation. Hence the argument to increase taxes. However, no gospel canon advocates going into debt to "help thy neighbor," nor is it generally taught that the works deserving of personal salvation can be assigned to a third-party proxy like government. Since the United States Constitution clearly separates both church and state, people must bridle their expectations for government to "do it all" at the expense of self-reliance. Government's first mandate is to protect, not provide; to ensure everyone can play the game, not pay for participation lest the game becomes too expensive to host! In extreme cases government may establish safety nets but only if national security is paid for first and the country can still maintain fiscal solvency afterward.

By fighting a socially charged archetype like poverty with blunt federal spending, President Johnson created high inflation—meaning it took more money to buy the same product because people were unsure of the future—which repels business activity. A loaf of bread may cost a dollar now and two dollars in twenty years, but what if it doubled in price tomorrow? Government and stable pricing are the road businesses drive on. Speed bumps and cracks in the asphalt are typical. Reasonable regulation and moderate taxes are expected. However, it is only when uncertainty abounds that drivers tend to pull over. With high inflation comes a declining value of money, and companies may only drive a few hundred feet for short-term financial certainties rather than embarking on multi-day road trips that end in innovation for long-term gains.

The overwhelming budget deficit from Johnson's model of spending his way out of poverty, coupled with the cost of the Vietnam War, pushed inflation to its highest rate in eighteen years. After Johnson came Richard Nixon, who expanded entitlement spending even faster by 20 percent.[4]

The rest of the decade after 1974 saw an unprecedented average rate of inflation over 8 percent. Both Presidents Ford and Carter tackled inflation by trying to persuade the American people to change their lifestyle—to drive less, to grow their own vegetables, to heat their homes less, and to stop being wasteful. If demand for products declined, they believed prices would follow suit. This was clearly a last attempt but a typical one from government: artificially create the fruits of effective policy without addressing the real problem. America needed its confidence back, and selling the virtues of self-sacrifice while politicians continued their spending spree wouldn't work.

By the end of the 1970s, the country's mood was dismal. Inflation contributed significantly, fueled by federal overspending and a nine-fold increase in the price of oil imported from countries hostile to American ideals. The 1970s were plagued by other disheartening events. Greenspan and Wooldridge do a good job of summarizing the conditions of the decade. Richard Nixon resigned as president. Gerald Ford and Jimmy Carter were both voted out of office after a single term. America lost the Vietnam War. City populations were shrinking as inhabitants fled unemployment and high murder rates. Richard Nixon worried in private that the United States had "become subject to the decadence which eventually destroys a civilization."[5] *Time* magazine published a cover story asking, "Can Capitalism Survive?"[6] Business growth and productivity declined. During the 1970s, the proportion of Americans who said that they "trust the federal government" fell from 75 percent to 25 percent,[7] and the stock market had declined by 37 percent.

AMERICA BOUNCES
BACK

•••••••••••

How did America pull itself out of the 1970s rut and leap from questioning its own survival to achieving low unemployment, low inflation, GDP growth, and record-breaking gains in the stock market just eight years later?

During the 1800s, government constrained itself to simply protecting the American economy so people could work out their own success. However, from the 1930s through the 1970s, government's scope expanded to generating prosperity too. Ironically, state activism made things worse. FDR's New Deal increased the unemployment rate and Johnson's Great Society suffocated market growth such that the Dow closed at exactly the same level where it was ten years previous (838.74 in 1979 versus 838.92 in 1970).

Taking office in 1981, President Ronald Reagan believed the people would be better served if business retook the economic driver's seat. In his inaugural address Reagan stated, "In the present crisis government is not the solution to our problem; government is the problem." Government is the stool to stand on, not the ladder to climb. Reagan's favorite president was Calvin Coolidge "because he had been so silent, keeping the hand of the federal government out of the conduct of society and allowing business to prosper throughout the twenties."[1] The Reagan administration treated the country like a business, accepting unpopular costs up front to achieve superior gains later. "There are simple answers," Reagan liked to say, "just no easy ones."

He imposed a hiring freeze on the entire federal workforce and proposed budget cuts, and the Federal Reserve raised interest rates to beat inflation. But the capstone to Reagan's agenda was personal income tax cuts from 70 percent to 24 percent, which the 1990 budget report concluded cost $613 billion. What does this cost mean? Critics refer to it as the money government will no longer receive to pay for benefits that were promised to the people. That concern is legitimate, but Reagan's alternate view addresses this: it's a down payment for greater tax revenues in the future from improved economic growth.

Opponents typically bemoan tax cuts by defending the former definition over the latter, but would anyone turn down a better paying job for the sake of keeping the smaller paycheck they're already used to? Social spending obligations should never hold growth policies hostage.

Reagan favored the investment narrative and was willing to incur the cost of economic expansion via tax cuts over funding the status quo. Why?

For the same reason a baby needs its mother. An infant cannot sustain itself, nor can the government. Reagan believed in the power of business to create wealth and believed that government feeds off its fruits. Therefore, businesses must succeed for government benefits to continue. As President Kennedy aphoristically stated in 1963, "a rising tide lifts all boats" —including the government yacht! However, if the weight of deficits still appears to be sinking the ship, then alleviating the load through spending cuts, rather than lowering the water level through tax hikes, proves to be a more effective approach for staying afloat.

Were Reagan's policies a good investment for the country?

An almost euphoric economic condition ensued. It is estimated that by 1989, asset values including stocks, bonds, and real estate went up by more than $5 trillion.[2] Given the $613 billion cost of tax cuts, that's a 715 percent return in the same decade! Tax cuts are a double-edged sword. Too steep, and the government won't have enough money to protect the county. Too shallow, and the economy will remain disincentivized to innovate for growth. Reagan found the sweet spot in between. Real federal revenue adjusted for inflation was 19 percent higher than when he first took office,[3] and the Dow more than doubled. Annual GDP growth peaked over 7 percent, the poverty rate fell, and 18.7 million jobs had been created. One *Forbes* article said this growth was the equivalent of adding the West German economy to the US one.[4]

Clearly, government policy has the power to influence economic success. Prosperity for all is a hidden destination whose port can be found only by a country willing to sail under strict orders. The voyage begins with a stable currency. This is government's responsibility. It continues with a free-market system that allows businesses to keep most of their profits. With increasing profits, businesses can pay better wages and the ship reaches safe harbor. Wealth creation must precede its distribution. Reagan set America on this heading with zeal, and profitable productivity displaced personal poverty. In contrast, Johnson's Great Society set sail with a dropped anchor by paying for increased benefits out of pocket rather than creating conditions for them to pay for themselves. Such a course will invariably repeat the malaise of the 1970s.

The twentieth century ended with the same fervor as 1989. President Bill Clinton maintained the pro-business agenda with relative consistency. Through the end of the 1990s, America became the center of the high-tech industry, with the PC revolution and other innovations that entrepreneurs developed. The free market naturally progresses on its own. With compounding corporate confidence, the Dow hit record highs in every year of Clinton's presidency, while the government saw surpluses four years in a row from 1998 through 2001.

FINAL THOUGHTS

• • • • • • • • • • • •

Our friend the tortoise can finish his observations with the end of the twentieth century. It is easier to be objective with a distant past than a polarizing present. After a few hundred years, what can he conclude about prosperity and the role government plays?

America, in particular, has a centralized rule of law, but not a centralized economic plan. Though painstaking to pursue, wealth in any nation is proven to find those who apply the formula:

Wealth = Value x Volume

A person's wealth equals the value he provides multiplied by the number of people willing to pay for it. "God left us the world unfinished for man to work his skill upon. He left the electricity in the cloud, the oil in the earth. He left the rivers unbridged and the forests unfelled and the cities unbuilt. God gives to man the challenge of raw materials, not the ease of finished things. He leaves the pictures unpainted and the music unsung and the problems unsolved, that man might know the joys and glories of creation."[1]

The wealthy solve problems. Henry Ford developed the automobile, which decreased travel time and increased the capacity for delivery. Practically everyone was willing to replace their horse for it, and Ford became one of the richest men in the world. In contrast, salaried employees typically provide only the skill set for one supervisor. The pay is lower—value multiplied by volume. No matter the case to place blame for the past, fate honors what you do now. Only in America is failure widely tolerated as a sign of ambition. The most toxic mind-set governs decision-making by what you think you are owed as a result of systemic injustice. Victims of circumstance rarely identify as victors.

Does the existence of one wealthy person preclude the ability of another to gain the same?

In 1980 the average salary of the boss of a Fortune 500 company was forty times as much as a factory worker. By 2000 it was 475 times as much,[2] but median household income also grew from $17,710 to $41,990 during the same time.[3] In the end, few would forfeit more than double their income just to spite the rising pay of executives. Economic mobility is a far better measure of justice that income equality. Since wealth creation cannot exist without a value-add, the term "concentration of wealth" implies value can only be produced by a select few. How self-defeating to believe your ability to develop new skills is automatically hindered by the amount of money other people have! Resenting the wealth of others vilifies the free choice of the patrons they served.

Greenspan and Wooldridge highlight the living conditions of one hundred years ago to help curb the tendency to begrudge. In the year 1900, people spent fifty-eight hours per week on household chores,[4] indoor plumbing didn't exist so each family carried an average of nine thousand gallons of water to and from their house each year,[5] the average worker toiled sixty hours per week,[6] and most people enjoyed only two annual holidays.

Today, only eighteen hours per week are spent on chores[4], running water is standard while lifespans have doubled,[5] and the average employee works forty hours per week, with eight national holidays and two weeks paid vacation. Indeed, the majority of citizens in America already enjoy the living conditions of the top 1 percent compared to previous generations by virtue of the technological and medical advances that have taken place. Given the country's economic activity before the first World War, it is unreasonable to now expect more aggressive benefit programs that pay out above what the market naturally provides.

Still, the debate for how to create prosperity seems to persist between two options: free markets or centralized planning. World history sheds an unfavorable light on the latter. Communist East Germany had achieved only a third of the productivity of the capitalist West Germany.[7] There were a stubborn many who wanted to try again, but eventually objective awareness could not be ignored. Greenspan and Wooldridge quote an Indian official keen on communist ideals who recalled, "Between the fall of the Berlin Wall in 1989 and the collapse of the Soviet Union in 1991, I felt as though I were awakening from a thirty-five-year dream. Everything I have believed about economic systems and had tried to implement was wrong."[8]

History is the best teacher, and after watching countless world and American chronicles, this is the conclusion our friend the tortoise has reached: that free-market economies serve society with greater financial and social progress than centralized economies. Why?

Free markets by definition are "free" from government planning. The needs of the people are met by businesses willing to fill the void for profit. Obviously, this potential for wealth attracts numerous suitors who take risk to innovate solutions. Business competition ensures the best products win the most customers at affordable prices. At the same time, political competition ensures the candidate with the best plan for public service wins the most votes. Competition complements the common good, as freedom of choice incentivizes the best options to be widely available.

This construct is foreign to most countries and hinges on the principle that "you keep what you grow." Free markets pay the people more than the state. Taxes are low. Efficiency is measured by how much output is delivered above the cost of inputs to create it. With greater efficiencies, the market responds with further incentive to innovate. The means and gains of production remain outside of government autonomy. This is what "power to the people" refers to: control of production so their needs are not held hostage by government fiat. A business owner controls what his business does. An employee controls what he spends his paycheck on. Peaceful persuasion, then, becomes the only tool at government's disposal to attempt wealth diversion from the private sector to public policy. In the end, the best litmus test for public political freedom is the private profitable business.

Centralized market systems by definition concentrate economic authority. In essence, government is its own business and the citizenry, its employees. Businesses serve as extensions of the parent bureaucracy. The country's natural resources are annexed as government property. The needs of the people are met with guaranteed basic necessities from the state, but pursuit of any further personal happiness represents a cost to the common good. Government owns both the means and gains of production. Consequently, need becomes the currency of survival instead of the validation to innovate. There is neither competition in business nor in politics, yielding a lack of incentives to produce better alternatives. Standards of living stagnate, failing to keep pace with the technological advances of the rest of the world. The common catchphrase of this philosophy is "from each according to his ability, to each according to his needs." Centralized economies pay the state more than the people. Efficiency is measured by dependency, which politicians view as the unbiased unifier that fuels acceptance of their utopian ideals.

However, with greater dependence, subservient citizens respond with less motivation to extend their own effort beyond what is expected to avoid punishment. Resentment replaces gratitude since people tend to value more what could have been that what actually is. The business owner is told what to sell and for how much. The value of hard-working employees is taken and then redistributed through government programs, which is the same as lending money to a friend in need: don't expect anything back. As greater portions of income are confiscated, persuasion loses priority. Political agendas morph into forced mandates rather than debated proposals. The earliest warning signs of this extractive mind-set appear "under the radar" as good intentions from a government with open arms.

Which "island" would you prefer to live on?

Equality of opportunity to work as you wish, yielding uneven financial results? Or equality of result regardless of the work you do?

Children rarely maintain the same excitement for presents received just a few weeks prior. Regardless of how much the government provides, eventually the people will think they can do better on their own. Politicians would do well to remember that allowing the pursuit of self-interest is the greatest deterrent against revolt. The magic of free markets is also the social progress they manage to sustain, since the changing needs of the people determine how business evolves to stay competitive.

Let us assume for the moment that the lessons of history do not apply today. That circumstances warrant a change. That government's role should be to intervene, to provide for the people, and to serve as the engine of progress. We should be wary of any institution that has operated at a net loss 85 percent of the time since 1929, as the American government has. Any political entity that does not prioritize cost minimization because of belief in a cause no matter the expense is on a road that ends with human rights violations. The more authority government uses to provide, the more power it has to take away what was given. Hence, personal accountability is the most sustainable business model: to not consume more value than you create. Markets will fluctuate, stressing the need to diversify skill sets that can be applied to multiple industries. Don't blame technological progress for your failure to adapt. It's not the mechanic's fault that horse-shoes don't substitute for car tires.

My family, I urge you to develop a pioneering spirit. The credo that maximizes your potential treats prosperity as a learned skill, not as an occurrence of happenstance. Nor is prosperity a debt to be claimed from government simply because you're a citizen. Sustenance from the state is saltwater that cannot satisfy in the long run. Rather, take responsibility for your own success, and widen your view of possibilities to pursue. In the words of Mark Twain, "Twenty years from now you will be more disappointed by the things that you didn't do than by the ones you did do. So throw off the bowlines. Sail away from the safe harbor. Catch the trade winds in your sails. Explore. Dream. Discover."

REFERENCES

•••••••••••

PART I – THE SIX RULES OF GOVERNMENT

Rule Number One

1. Daron Acemoglu and James A. Robinson, *Why Nations Fail: The Origins of Power, Prosperity, and Poverty* (New York: Random House, 2012), 133.

2. Ibid., 133–6.

3. Ibid., 238–41.

Rule Number Two

1. Presidential debate, Oct. 28, 1980

2. Daron Acemoglu and James A. Robinson, *Why Nations Fail: The Origins of Power, Prosperity, and Poverty* (New York: Random House, 2012), 73.

3. Ibid., 389.

4. "Kim Jong-un's Unbelievable Life of Luxury." December 27, 2016, www.msn.com.

Rule Number Three

1. Daron Acemoglu and James A. Robinson, *Why Nations Fail: The Origins of Power, Prosperity, and Poverty* (New York: Random House, 2012), 284.

2. Ibid., 87–88.

3. Julia Limitone, "Taxes drive New Yorkers to Florida by the Truckload in Just a Decade." Fox Business. August 19, 2019. www.foxbusiness.com.

4. Brittany De Lea, Economist Reacts to High Numbers of New Yorkers Fleeing to Florida Because of High State Taxes. July 25, 2019, Fox News

5. Editorial Board, "Connecticut's Tax Roulette," *Wall Street Journal*, May 8, 2019.

6. Bob Stefanowski, "Connecticut's Blue Politicians Spill an Ocean of Red Ink," *Wall Street Journal*, June 15, 2019.

7. Editorial Board, "A Connecticut Tax Story," *Wall Street Journal*, June 19, 2019.

8. Daron Acemoglu and James A. Robinson, *Why Nations Fail: The Origins of Power, Prosperity, and Poverty* (New York: Random House, 2012), 337–8.

9. Ibid., 373–6.

10. Ibid., 152–6.

Rule Number Four

1. Kaylee Greenlee, "Sorry, AOC and Bernie Sanders: Scandanavia is no Socialist Paradise," *National Interest*, July 27, 2019, www.nationalinterest.org.

2. Nima Sanandaji, "5 Myths About Nordic Socialism Peddled by the Left," September 6, 2016, www.stream.org.

3. Adam O'Neal, "Why Bernie Sanders Is Wrong About Sweden," *Wall Street Journal*, August 24, 2019.

4. Susanna Hoffman, "Socialism Didn't Work in Sweden and It Won't Work in America," *Federalist*, June 25, 2019.

5. Alan Greenspan and Adrian Wooldridge, *Capitalism in America: A History* (New York: Penguin Random House, 2018), 610.

6. Rainer Zitelmann, "The Myth of Nordic Socialism," *Barron's*, April 3, 2019.

7. Alan Greenspan and Adrian Wooldridge, *Capitalism in America: A History* (New York: Penguin Random House, 2018), 611.

8. Grace Donnelly, "Finland's Basic Income Experiment Will End in 2019," *Fortune*, April 19, 2018.

9. Heikki Hiilamo, "Disappointing results from the Finnish basic income experiment," February 8, 2019, www.helsinki.fi.

10. Paul Hannon, "Experiment in Finland With Guaranteed Income Creates Less Stress but No Jobs," *Wall Street Journal*, February 8, 2019.

11. Reuters, "Finland's Basic Income Trial Boosts Happiness, but Not Employment," *New York Times*, February 9, 2019.

12. Angus Maddison, *Monitoring the World Economy, 1820–1992* (Paris: Organization for Economic Cooperation and Development, 1995).

13. Elvis Picardo, "The Origins of Greece's Debt Crisis," October 8, 2018, www.investopedia.com.

14. John Nic. Yfantopoulos, The Welfare State in Greece

15. Phillip Inman, "A Decade of Overspending: How Greece Plunged Into Economic Crisis," *Guardian*, July 3, 2015.

16. Prokopis Hatzinikolaou, Dramatic drop in budget revenues. February 7, 2012

17. "Labor Force Survey: May 2012," Piraeus: Hellenic Statistical Authority, August 9, 2012.

18. Nektaria Stamouli, "Greece's Prospects Remain Bleak, Whoever Governs," *Wall Street Journal*, July 6, 2019.

19. Nektaria Stamouli, "Many Greeks Struggle to Keep Their Heads Above Water as Bailout Ends," *Wall Street Journal*, August 20, 2018.

20. Margaret Coker, "Calls to Overhaul Kuwait's Welfare System Grow Louder," *Wall Street Journal*, October 30, 2013.

21. WikiLeaks, "Cablegate: From Cradle-to-Grave: An Overview of Kuwait's Welfare" May 1, 2006, www.scoop.co.nz.

22. Sylvia Westall, "Kuwait's PM Says Welfare State is 'Unsustainable,' Calls for Cuts," Reuters, October 28, 2013.

23. Yaroslav Trofimov, "Kuwait Shows Dept of Opposition Towards Austerity in the Gulf," *Wall Street Journal*, January 5, 2017.

Rule Number Five

1. Daron Acemoglu and James A. Robinson, *Why Nations Fail: The Origins of Power, Prosperity, and Poverty* (New York: Random House, 2012), 277–9.

2. Ibid., 104.

3. Ibid., 263.

4. History Hit, "What Was Stalin's Controversial First Five Year Plan?" October 1, 2016, www.historyhit.com.

5. Oleg V. Khlevniuk, *Stalin: New Biography of a Dictator* (New Haven, CT: Yale University Press, 2015).

6. Martin Sixsmith, *Russia: A 1,000-Year Chronicle of the Wild East* (New York: Harry N. Abrams, 2014).

7. Viktor Yushchenko, "The Holodomor," *Wall Street Journal*, November 26, 2007.

8. Patrick J. Kiger, "How Joseph Stalin Starved Millions in the Ukrainian Famine," April 16, 2019, www.history.com.

9. Robert Conquest, *The Harvest of Sorrow: Soviet Collectivization and the Terror-Famine* (New York: Oxford University Press,1986).

10. Sheila Fitzpatrick, The Question of Social Support for Collectivization. 2010

11. "Seventeen Moments in Soviet History," June 17, 2015, www.soviethistory.msu.edu.

12. Stephen Hansen, *Time and Revolution: Marxism and the Design of Soviet Institutions* (Chapel Hill: University of North Carolina Press, 1997) 95.

13. Nikita Khrushchev, *Memoirs of Nikita Khrushchev* (2004).

14. Joshua Keefe, "Stalin and the Drive to Industrialize the Soviet Union," *Inquiries* 1, no.1 (2009), www.inquiriesjournal.com.

15. Bruce F. Pauley, *Hitler, Stalin, and Mussolini: Totalitarianism in the Twentieth Century* (New York: Wiley-Blackwell, 2014).

16. 1988 U.S. Congressional commission report.

17. Alex de Waal, Executive Director - World Peace Foundation, Tufts University.

18. Mikhail Sergeevich Gorbachev, *Manifesto for the Earth: Action Now for Peace, Global Justice, and a Sustainable Future* (West Sussex, UK: Clairview Books, 2006).

19. Oleg V. Khlevniuk, *Stalin: New Biography of a Dictator* (New Haven, CT: Yale University Press, 2015)

20. Robert Conquest, *The Great Terror: A Reassessment* (New York: Oxford University Press: 1971).

21. Daron Acemoglu and James A. Robinson, *Why Nations Fail: The Origins of Power, Prosperity, and Poverty* (New York: Random House, 2012), 130.

22. Ibid., 131.

23. Ibid., 127.

24. Patrick J. Kiger, "How Venezuela Fell from the Richest Country in South America into Crisis," May 9, 2019, www.history.com.

25. Geri Smith, "A Food Fight for Hugo Chávez," *Bloomberg Businessweek*, March 11, 2010.

26. Colleen Walsh, "Understanding Venezuela's Collapse," *Harvard Gazette*, February 12, 2019.

27. Juan Feraro, "In Venezuela, Land 'Rescue' Hopes Unmet," *Washington Post*, June 20, 2009.

28. Associated Press, "Hugo Chavez Nationalizes Cement Industry," CBS News, April 4, 2008, www.cbsnews.com.

29. Associated Press, "Outraged Chávez Puts Stop to Near-Complete Shopping Mall," *Guardian*, December 24, 2008.

30. "Venezuela Nationalizes Steel Industry," CNN Money, May 1, 2008, https://money.cnn.com.

31. Associated Press, "Chavez Seizes Venezuelan Rice Plants," *Wall Street Journal*, updated March 2, 2009.

32. Mark Weisbrot, Rebecca Ray, and Luis Sandoval, "The Chávez Administration at 10 Years: The Economy and Social Indicators," Washington, DC: Center for Economic and Policy Research, February 2009.

33. Central Intelligence Agency, The World Factbook 1998: Venezuela, 1998, https://cia.gov.

34. mltpl, www.multpl.com/venezuela-gdp-growth-rate/table/by-year.

35. Max Fisher and Amanda Taub, "How Venezuela Went From the Richest Economy in South America to the Brink of Financial Ruin," *Independent*, May 21, 2017, www.independent.co.uk.

36. "Hugo Chavez," *Wall Street Journal*, March 7, 2013.

37. Thor Halvorssen, "A Rotting Chicken in Every Pot: Venezuela's Disastrous Food Policy," *Huffington Post*, August 2, 2010.

38. "Producción de cemento bajó 60 percent por paralización de hornos," *La Patilla*, May 31, 2013.

39. Associated Press, "Power Cut Paralyses Venezuela," *Guardian*, September 4, 2013.

40. "Cae producción de acero y aluminio en Venezuela durante 2014," Reuters, March 23, 2015.

41. Santiago Pérez, "Venezuela's Economic Collapse Explained in 9 Charts," *Wall Street Journal*, March 25, 2019.

42. Anatoly Kurmanaev, "Venezuela's Collapse is the Worst Outside of War in Decades, Economists Say," *New York Times*, May 17, 2019.

43. Jonathan Mirsky, "The China We Don't Know," *New York Review of Books*, February 26, 2009.

44. Nicholas R. Lardy and John K. Fairbank, "The Chinese Economy Under Stress, 1958–1965," in *The Cambridge History of China*, eds. Roderick MacFarquhar, John K. Fairbank (Cambridge: Cambridge University Press, 1987), 360–97.

45. Ibid., 368.

46. Lee Edwards, "The Legacy of Mao Zedong is Mass Murder," The Heritage Foundation, February 2, 2010, https://heritage.org.

47. Frank Dikötter, *Mao's Great Famine: The History of China's Most Devastating Catastrophe, 1958–62*. (New York: Bloomsbury, 2010) 39.

48. William Hinton, *Shenfan: The Continuing Revolution in a Chinese Village* (New York: Random House, 1984), 236–45.

49. Frank Dikötter, *Mao's Great Famine: The History of China's Most Devastating Catastrophe, 1958–62*. (New York: Bloomsbury, 2010) 33.

50. Ibid.

51. William Hinton, *Shenfan: The Continuing Revolution in a Chinese Village* (New York: Random House, 1984), 234–40, 247–9.

52. Richard Bernstein, "Horror of a Hidden Chinese Famine," *New York Times*, February 5, 1997.

53. Tania Branigan, "China's Great Famine: The True Story," *Guardian*, January 1, 2013.

54. Frank Dikötter, *Mao's Great Famine: The History of China's Most Devastating Catastrophe, 1958–62*. (New York: Bloomsbury, 2010) 294–6.

55. Jiayang Fan, "Yan Lianke's Forbidden Satires of China," *New Yorker*, October 8, 2018, www.newyorker.com.

56. Frank Dikötter, "Mao's Great Leap to Famine," *New York Times*, December 15, 2010.

57. Frank Dikötter, *Mao's Great Famine: The History of China's Most Devastating Catastrophe, 1958–62*. (New York: Bloomsbury, 2010) 333.

58. William Harms, "China's Great Leap Forward," *University of Chicago Chronicle* 15, no. 13 (March 14, 1996).

Rule Number Six

1. Edward P. Lazear, "Want to Reduce Inequality? Consult China, Vietnam, and India," *Wall Street Journal*, March 31, 2015.

2. Andreas Bergh and Magnus Henrekson, "Lessons from the Swedish Welfare State," *Wall Street Journal*, July 10, 2010.

3. Michael Saltsman, "How San Francisco Is Killing Its Restaurants," *Wall Street Journal*, October 18, 2019.

4. Neal McCluskey and Diego Zuluaga, "The Worst Federal Student-Loan Program," *Wall Street Journal*, April 10, 2019.

5. Editorial Board, "Cryptocurrency to the Rescue," *Wall Street Journal*, July 18, 2019.

6. Johnny Munkhammar, "The Swedish Model," *Wall Street Journal*, January 26, 2011.

7. Michael Munger, "How Capitalism Saved Sweden from the Evils of Socialism," Capitalist Magazine, March 27, 2019.

8. C. Fred Bergsten, "The Swedish Model for Economic Recovery," August 30, 2013, www.piie.com.

9. Jesús Fernández-Villaverde and Lee E. Ohanian, "How Sweden Overcame Socialism," *Wall Street Journal*, January 9, 2019.

10. Rainer Zitelmann, "The Myth of Nordic Socialism," *Barron's*, April 3, 2019.

11. António Caeiro, *Pela China Dentro* (Dom Quixote, 2005).

12. Michael Meyer, "The Quiet Revolt That Saved China," *Wall Street Journal*, April 16, 2019.

13. Michael Hunt, *The World Transformed: 1945 to the Present* (New York: Oxford University Press, 2016), 355.

14. Leonard Silk, "Economic Scene; The Open Door Policy in China," *New York Times*, September 27, 1985.

15. Wei Ge, *Special Economic Zones and the Economic Transition in China* (London: World Scientific Publishing, 1999).

16. Loren Brandt, Thomas G. Rawski, and John Sutton, "China's Industrial Development," in

China's Great Economic Transformation, eds. Loren Brandt and Thomas G. Rawski (Cambridge: Cambridge University Press, 2008), 573.

17. Peter Engardio, "China Is a Private-Sector Economy," *Bloomberg Businessweek*, August 21, 2005.

18. Abraham Denmark, "40 Years Ago, Deng Xiaoping Changed China—and the World," *Washington Post*, December 12, 2018.

19. Alan Taylor, *American Colonies* (New York: Penguin Random House, 2002), 25.

20. Marianne Ward and John Devereux, "Measuring British Decline: Direct Versus Long-Span Income Measures," *Journal of Economic History* 63, no. 3 (September 2003): 826–51.

21. Alan Greenspan and Adrian Wooldridge, *Capitalism in America: A History* (New York: Penguin Random House, 2018), 138.

22. Ibid., 128.

23. Better Life Index, "Income," www.oecdbetterlifeindex.org.

24. Alicia Adamczyk, "The US is home to more billionaires than China, Germany and Russia Combined," CNBC, May 9, 2019, www.cnbc.com.

PART II – Government vs. Business: The Two "Islands" in America

America's Early Days

1. Alan Greenspan and Adrian Wooldridge, *Capitalism in America: A History* (New York: Penguin Random House, 2018), 128.

2. Ibid., 185.

3. Ibid., 150.

4. Ibid., 119.

5. Ibid., 82.

6. Ibid., 75.

A Shift in Attitude

1. Hugh Rockoff, "Until It's Over, Over There: The US Economy in World War I," in *The Economics of World War I* , eds. Stephen Broadberry and Mark Harrison (Cambridge: Cambridge University Press, 2005).

The Roaring Twenties

1. Alan Greenspan and Adrian Wooldridge, *Capitalism in America: A History* (New York: Penguin Random House, 2018), 264.

2. David M. Kennedy, *Freedom and Fear: The American People in Depression and War, 1929–1945* (New York: Oxford University Press, 1999), 30.

3.   Duplex Printing Press Co. v. Deering, 254 U.S. 443 (1921).

4.   Adkins v. Children's Hospital, 261 U.S. 525 (1923).

5.   Alan Greenspan and Adrian Wooldridge, *Capitalism in America: A History* (New York: Penguin Random House, 2018),

6.   Anthony Mayo and Nitin Nohria, *In Their Time: The Greatest Business Leaders of the Twentieth Century* (New York: Harvard Business Review Press, 2005), 87.

7.   Adolf Berle and Gardiner Means, *The Modern Corporation and Private Property*, (City: Publisher, Year) 60.

The Great Depression

1.   Claude S. Fischer, *Made in America: A Social History of American Culture and Character* (Chicago: University of Chicago Press, 2010), 68.

2.   David M. Kennedy, *Freedom and Fear: The American People in Depression and War, 1929–1945* (New York: Oxford University Press, 1999), 77.

3.   Alan Greenspan and Adrian Wooldridge, *Capitalism in America: A History* (New York: Penguin Random House, 2018), 333.

4.   Ibid., 355.

5. William Leuchtenburg, *The American President: From Teddy Roosevelt to Bill Clinton* (New York: Oxford University Press, 2015), 157.

6. John F. Cogan, *The High Cost of Good Intentions: A History of US Federal Entitlement Programs* (Stanford, CA: Stanford University Press, 2017), 93.

7. Burton Folsom Jr., *New Deal or Raw Deal? How FDRs Economic Legacy Has Damaged America* (New York: Simon & Schuster, 2008), 2.

Recovery

1. Robert Gordon, *The Rise and Fall of American Growth: The US Standard of Living Since the Civil War* (Princeton, NJ: Princeton University Press, 2016), 536.

2. Ibid., 646.

3. David M. Kennedy, *Freedom and Fear: The American People in Depression and War, 1929–1945* (New York: Oxford University Press, 1999), 283.

4. Alan Greenspan and Adrian Wooldridge, *Capitalism in America: A History* (New York: Penguin Random House, 2018), 379.

5. James T. Patterson, *Grand Expectations: The United States, 1945–1974* (New York: Oxford University Press, 1996), 139.

6.   Robert Gordon, *The Rise and Fall of American Growth: The US Standard of Living Since the Civil War* (Princeton, NJ: Princeton University Press, 2016), 466.

7.   Ibid., 390.

The 1970s: From Gold to Lead

1.   Alan Greenspan and Adrian Wooldridge, *Capitalism in America: A History* (New York: Penguin Random House, 2018), 421.

2.   Lyndon B. Johnson, May 22, 1964.

3.   Alan Greenspan and Adrian Wooldridge, *Capitalism in America: A History* (New York: Penguin Random House, 2018), 423.

4.   Ibid., 424–5.

5.   Steven F. Hayward, *The Age of Reagan: The Fall of the Old Liberal Order, 1964–1980* (New York: Random House, 2001), 321.

6.   Alan Greenspan and Adrian Wooldridge, *Capitalism in America: A History* (New York: Penguin Random House, 2018), 417.

7.   Ibid., 423–4.

America Bounces Back

1.   Anthony Mayo and Nitin Nohria, *In Their Time: The Greatest Business Leaders of the Twentieth Century*

(New York: Harvard Business Review Press, 2005), 292.

2. Martin Anderson, "The Reagan Boom — Greatest Ever," *New York Times*, January 17, 1990.

3. Phil Gramm and Mike Solon, "Reagan Cut Taxes, Revenue Boomed," *Wall Street Journal*, August 3, 2017.

4. Kyle Smith, "Sorry, Obama Fans: Reagan Did Better on Jobs and Growth," *Forbes*, September 11, 2014.

Final Thoughts

1. Thomas S. Monson, "In Quest of the Abundant Life," 1988, www.churchofjesuschrist.org.

2. Alan Greenspan and Adrian Wooldridge, *Capitalism in America: A History* (New York: Penguin Random House, 2018), 467.

3. US Census Bureau, Table H-6, "Regions by Median & Mean Income, All Races," www.census.gov.

4. Alan Greenspan and Adrian Wooldridge, *Capitalism in America: A History* (New York: Penguin Random House, 2018), 598–9.

5. Ibid., 596.

6. Ibid., 597.

7. Ibid., 522.

8. Daniel Yergin and Joseph Stanislaw, *The Commanding Heights: The Battle Between Government and the Marketplace That Is Remaking the Modern World* (New York: Simon & Schuster, 1998), 168.

CPSIA information can be obtained
at www.ICGtesting.com
Printed in the USA
BVHW031726130120
569395BV00001B/11/P

9 781734 308402